S. Russell Forbes

Rambles in Naples

an archaeological and historical guide to the museums, galleries, churches, and

antiquities of Naples and its environs

S. Russell Forbes

Rambles in Naples

an archaeological and historical guide to the museums, galleries, churches, and antiquities of Naples and its environs

ISBN/EAN: 9783337180522

Printed in Europe, USA, Canada, Australia, Japan

Cover: Foto ©Andreas Hilbeck / pixelio.de

More available books at **www.hansebooks.com**

VIEW OF NAPLES FROM VIRGIL'S TOMB.

Rambles in Naples.

An Archæological and Historical Guide

TO THE

MUSEUMS, GALLERIES, VILLAS, CHURCHES,
AND ANTIQUITIES OF NAPLES
AND ITS ENVIRONS.

By

S. RUSSELL FORBES, PH.D.,
Archæological and Historical Lecturer on Roman Antiquities;
Author of "Rambles in Rome," "The Footsteps of St. Paul in Rome,"
"The Holy City—Jerusalem," Etc.

Fourth Edition, Enlarged,
With Maps, Plans, and Illustrations.

London:
T. NELSON AND SONS, PATERNOSTER ROW.
EDINBURGH; AND NEW YORK.

ROME: S. R. FORBES, 93 VIA BABUINO.
NAPLES: F. FURCHHEIM, Bookseller, 59 PIAZZA DEI MARTIRI.

1893.

*Entered at Stationers' Hall, London, and
Registered in accordance with the requirements of the Italian Law.*

Preface.

THIS little work is offered to the public as the result of excursions actually carried out by the author, that others may benefit by his experience.

The want of a practical, handy, reliable guide has been long felt by visitors to Naples; and this is offered as a companion to our popular "Rambles in Rome." In this, the same system has been adopted: thus those visitors who make a long stay in this delightful neighbourhood can divide the Rambles to suit their convenience, and those who make a shorter visit can select the things most likely to interest them.

S. R. F.

NAPLES, *October 1892.*

List of Illustrations.

VIEW OF NAPLES FROM VIRGIL'S TOMB,	*Frontispiece*
MONTE CASSINO,	3
PLAN OF GROUND FLOOR OF NATIONAL MUSEUM,	11
CAVE CANEM,	12
BREAD FOUND AT POMPEII,	26
FOUNTAIN IN THE VILLA NAZIONALE,	41
MAP OF POMPEII,	45
SKETCH MAP OF THE REGIONI OF POMPEII,	53
PLASTER CAST OF HUMAN BODY,	54
TEMPLE OF VENUS,	55
THE FORUM,	57
TEMPLE OF JUPITER,	59
TRIANGULAR FORUM AND TEMPLE OF HERCULES,	61
THE AMPHITHEATRE, POMPEII,	65
CAMPANI VICTORIA,	66
PUBLIC BATHS AT POMPEII,	70
THE TEPIDARIUM,	71
THE CALIDARIUM,	72
THE FRIGIDARIUM,	73
HOUSE OF THE TRAGIC POET,	75
PLAN OF THE HOUSE OF PANSA,	76
STREET OF SALLUST,	77
GATE OF HERCULANEUM, POMPEII,	78

STREET OF TOMBS,	80
VILLA OF DIOMEDES,	82
STREET OF THE BALCONY,	85
VESUVIUS BEFORE THE FIRST ERUPTION,	91
VESUVIUS IN ERUPTION,	93
THE GROTTO OF POSILIPO,	99
MOLE OF PUTEOLI,	102
TEMPLE OF SERAPIS,	105
BAY OF BAIÆ,	112
ISLAND OF CAPRI,	119
THE BLUE GROTTO,	121
SORRENTO,	123
CASTELLAMARE DI STABIA,	125
AMALFI,	127
TEMPLE OF CERES, PÆSTUM,	129
TEMPLE OF NEPTUNE, PÆSTUM,	131
PLAN OF PÆSTUM,	132

MAPS.

NAPLES,	between pages 6, 7
POMPEII,	53, 54
ENVIRONS,	134, 135

Contents.

ROME TO NAPLES.

THE ROUTE—RAILWAYS FROM NAPLES..........................1-6

RAMBLE I.

NAPLES—CASTELLO DELL' OVO—QUAY OF S. LUCIA—PIAZZA DEL PLEBISCITO—CHURCH OF S. FRANCESCO DI PAOLA—ROYAL PALACE—VIA ROMA—PIAZZA DANTE—NATIONAL MUSEUM—VILLA CAPODIMONTE—CHURCH OF S. GENNARO—CATACOMBS—GESU NUOVO—S. CHIARA—S. DOMENICO MAGGIORE—LA CAPPELLA DI S. SEVERO—S. ANNA DE' LOMBARDI—L'INCORONATA—PALAZZO FONDI—NEAPOLITAN LIFE...7-31

RAMBLE II.

PIAZZA DEI MARTIRI—THEATRE OF S. CARLO—PIAZZA DEL MUNICIPIO—CHURCH OF S. GIACOMO DEGLI SPAGNUOLI—FONTANA MEDINA—CASTEL NUOVO—TRIUMPHAL ARCH—CHURCH OF S. BARBARA—PORTA DEL CARMINE—S. MARIA DEL CARMINE—PIAZZA DEL MERCATO—CORSO GARIBALDI—PORTA CAPUANA—THE CEMETERIES—CASTEL CAPUANO—SS. APOSTOLI—S. PAOLO MAGGIORE, TEMPLE OF CASTOR AND POLLUX—THEATRE—S. LORENZO, BASILICA AUGUSTALIS—THE CATHEDRAL OF S. JANUARIUS, TEMPLE OF NEPTUNE—S. RESTITUTA, TEMPLE OF APOLLO—ANCIENT THEATRE(?)—S. MARTINO—CASTEL S. ELMO—CORSO VITTORIO EMANUELE—THE INTERNATIONAL HOSPITAL—VIRGIL'S TOMB—RIVIERA DI CHIAJA—VILLA NAZIONALE—THE AQUARIUM—IMPROVEMENTS.........................32-42

RAMBLE III.

TORRE DEL GRECO—TORRE DELL' ANNUNZIATA—POMPEII—HISTORICAL NOTICES—THE DESTRUCTION OF POMPEII—SYNOPSIS OF RAMBLE—IMPRESSIONS—CAMALDOLI...43-87

RAMBLE IV.

PORTICI—RESINA—VESUVIUS; HOW TO GET THERE; AND USEFUL HINTS—HISTORICAL NOTICES—HERCULANEUM—LA FAVORITA..88–97

RAMBLE V.

GROTTO OF POSILIPO—GROTTA DI CANE—LAGO D'AGNANO—ASTRONI—SOLFATARA—POZZUOLI—PAUL'S LANDING-PLACE—BRIDGE OF CALIGULA—TEMPLES OF SERAPIS, NEPTUNE, AND THE NYMPHS—CICERO'S VILLA—THEATRE—AMPHITHEATRE—MONTE NUOVO—ARCO FELICE—CUMÆ—GROTTO OF THE SIBYL—GROTTA DELLA PACE—LAKES AVERNUS AND LUCRINUS—TEMPLE OF APOLLO—GROTTA D'AVERNO—VIA HERCULEA—STUFE DI TRITONI—BATHS OF NERO—BAIÆ—TEMPLES OF DIANA, VENUS, AND MERCURY—LAKE FUSARO—AGRIPPINA'S TOMB—BACOLI—VILLA BAULI—CENTO CAMERELLE—PISCINA MIRABILIS—CAPO MISENO—ELYSIAN FIELDS—ISLAND OF NISIDA—GROTTO OF SEJANUS—VILLAS OF POLLIO AND LUCULLUS—SCHOOL OF VIRGIL...98–117

RAMBLE VI.

ISLAND OF CAPRI—HISTORICAL NOTICES—BLUE GROTTO—VILLAS OF TIBERIUS—SORRENTO—CASTELLAMARE—VIETRI—AMALFI—SALERNO—PÆSTUM..........113-134

VISITOR'S NEAPOLITAN DIRECTORY.

ARTISTS—BATHS—BANKERS—CARRIAGE FARES—CHEMISTS—CHURCHES (PROTESTANT)—CLUBS—CONSULATES—DINING-ROOMS, RESTAURANTS—DOCTORS—HOTELS—LIBRARIES AND BOOKSELLERS—MUSEUMS AND GALLERIES—MUSIC—NAVIGATION—OMNIBUSES AND TRAMWAYS—ORDERS REQUIRED, AND WHERE OBTAINABLE..135-141

NAPLES: HOW TO SEE IT.

So many visitors ask us to furnish them with an itinerary for seeing the principal objects in Naples and its neighbourhood in a few days, that we present the following, which we have often executed, and so know that it is practical.

Leave Rome by mid-day express, arriving in Naples in time for dinner. Take the omnibus to the hotel.

FIRST DAY.

Visit the Museum at 9 A.M. Lunch at the restaurant in the Galleria Principe di Napoli, opposite, at 12.30. After lunch, take a cab to the station, in time for the 2 o'clock express for Pompeii, with a return ticket. After seeing the ruined city, return to Naples by the evening train. Book places for the ascent of Vesuvius for the morrow at Cook's Office, Piazza dei Martiri.

SECOND DAY.

Carriage and funicular-rail excursion to the summit of Vesuvius, or, make the excursion by carriage to Pozzuoli and Baiæ.

THIRD DAY.

Steamboat excursion on the Bay of Naples to Capri. Visit the Blue Grotto, and, after lunch, take the steamer to Sorrento; land there, and take a carriage to Castellamare, by the celebrated road; thence by rail to Naples.

FOURTH DAY.

A carriage drive through the Via Roma up to the Church and Museum of S. Martino; hence along the Corso Vittorio Emanuele, noted for its splendid views, to the Grotto of Posilipo and Virgil's Tomb, returning to the hotel at 1 o'clock to dine. Leave in time for the afternoon fast express to Rome.

USEFUL HINTS.

On arrival, look sharply after your personal luggage, and get as quickly as possible into the omnibus of the hotel you have selected; then give the ticket of your registered baggage to the hotel porter, who will get it without your troubling.

If you take a cab to the hotel, refuse to proceed if a stranger mounts the box. " *Have him down !* " or you will have to pay a commission.

Pay no attention to touters at the railway.

Take lunch in the middle of the day.

If you get into a heat, do not go into the shade or into a building till you have cooled down.

On inhaling a bad odour, if the stomach is empty, take a nip of brandy, medicinally. Do not over-fatigue yourself.

THE NEW WATER SUPPLY TO NAPLES.

On May 10, 1885, King Humbert inaugurated the new water supply to the city of Naples, which has done more to improve the sanitary condition of Naples than anything else.

The sources are fifty miles from Naples, about a quarter of a mile from the Serino station on the railway between Naples and Avellino, at the fountains of Acquaro, Pelosi, Acquarolo, and Urcinolo, on the right of the Sabatto stream, covering a watershed of 40,000 square mètres. From here receiving channels take the water to a central reservoir 323 mètres above the sea, hence it is conducted to Cancello, and then to the reservoirs at Capodimonte. From there two channels take the water to the bottom of the Riviera di Chiaja, and three others supply the high parts of the city. The supply is two cubic mètres every two seconds, the flow being 1 m. 20 c. per second : 20,000 cubic mètres being sent to the high parts of the city, and 80,000 to the lower parts daily.

His Majesty, on inspecting the works for the new water supply, said, " This work is worthy of the ancient Romans, and has exceeded my expectations." The water is very pure and abundant, so that a long-standing reproach is now removed.

MAPS OF NAPLES AND POMPEII.

The numbers after our titles refer to the numbers on the maps, which show the exact location of the principal places of interest.

ROME TO NAPLES.

THE ROUTE.

A FEW notes on the route to Naples may not be unacceptable to our readers. We will presume that, being comfortably seated in the car, facing the engine, the train steams out of the Roman station, clear of which, on the right, are the remains of the Baths of Galliennus; we then shoot through the walls of Aurelian, and get a glimpse of the Porta Maggiore and the Baker's Tomb on the right. We then pass the junction of the Florence line on our left and the Pisa line on our right. On the left we get a peep of a picturesque piece of the Aqua Hadriana Aqueduct, covered with ivy and weeds, spanning the valley at right angles to the railway ; and we pass the Albano rail.

Then we run for some distance parallel with the Acqua Felice Aqueduct, and notice portions of the old Claudian Aqueduct, built of stone, with the brick *specus* of the Anio Novus on the top of it. At a short distance, parallel with it, is a piece of the Aqua Marcia, with the Tepula and Julia on the top. We cross the Frascati Road at Porta Furba, and on the left is Monte Grano, where the sculptured sarcophagus of the Capitoline Museum was found, and in it the Portland vase. Beyond, on the right, is the medieval Tor Fiscali, in the line of the Aqueduct. We here run parallel with the Felice Aqueduct, and, passing under it, trace the line of the Appian Way against the sky, on our right ; on our left is a fine long stretch of the Aqua Claudia, with some of its arches strengthened with the brickwork of Hadrian.

On the left are the extensive ruins of the Villa of Septimius Bassus (once a villa belonging to the Emperor Hadrian), the Sabine Hills, and Tivoli; whilst more to the front are Frascati and the Alban Hills. We run through Ciampino junction, where the line branches to the left, north of the Frascati line, the old Naples line running off to the right: that is now the Velletri-Terracina line. To the right is a fine view of Castel Gandolpho; then passing a twelfth century tower, we obtain an extensive view of Marino, Monte Cavo, and Rocca di Papa; and on the left, of the Campagna, Rome and its dome. We now run through a bed of lava, and see, to the right, the ruins of Borghetto, an extensive tenth century castle of the Savelli, on the Latin Way. Frascati then comes into the view, and we run through another lava bed. Below, on the left, is the drained basin of Lake Regillus, where Castor and Pollux fought for Rome. Tusculum occupies the ridge of the hill behind Frascati; beyond is Monte Porzio, so named from Cato the censor. Above is Monte Comprati. We then pass under Colonna, from which the princely house of Colonna derives its name. It represents the ancient city of Labicum, whose ruins are at *I Quadroni*. Strabo says it was fifteen miles from Rome, "now a small village possessed by a private individual. An ancient city now in ruins, situated on an eminence" (v. iii. 9). Cicero (*pro* Planc. ix.) alludes to its decayed state. Passing through a tunnel, the last town on the Alban Hills is Rocca Priora, which is situated on a lofty summit. To our left is an extensive view of the mountains of the Hernici. The next station is Zagarola, the ancient Scaptia. Here Gregory XIV. held the conference to revise the Vulgate edition of the Bible. Away to the left is Palestrina, the ancient Præneste, one of the earliest of the Italo-Greek cities. It was celebrated for its Temple of Fortune— Carneades the philosopher declaring that the most fortunate Fortune that he had seen was that of Præneste. Its site is now occupied by the Barberini Palace. The *arx* was on the top of the mountain above the town, 2,512 feet above the sea, and is now a hamlet called the Castel San Pietro, because it is said that S. Peter once dwelt there. Passing through a tunnel, we have some woods on the right, and then pass under the village of Labico. It is at the junction of the Labican and Latin Ways, which Strabo says was at Pictæ Tabernæ, twenty-eight miles from Rome. The railway now passes by Valmontone, with its vast palace of the Doria family, and issuing from a tunnel, we get a fine view of the town of Paliano, in front to the left, once an important Papal frontier fortress. It dates from the tenth century. On our right are the Volscian Alps. We pass through a short tunnel, and on our left have the ruined twelfth

MONTE CASSINO

century tower and walls of Piombinara; and we join the old Naples line at Segni station, which town is on a spur of the Volscian hills to the right, three and a half miles from the station. The town is 2,200 feet above the sea, and preserves a considerable extent of its massive polygonal walls, with its gates formed by converging blocks of stone, which support an architrave above.

Following the course of the Sacco, we pass medieval towers and Garvignano, on the right; Anagni station; then that of Sgurgola, with its medieval castle and walls, on the right. Here we skirt the base of the Volscian Alps, and passing Morolo, on the right, we enter the plain of the Tolero, past Ferentino (the Ferentinum of the Volscians, afterwards of the Hernici), which still retains its old walls The next stoppage is at Frosinone (the ancient Frusino); the Ceccano, with its fine stone bridge and palace, on the right; and beyond, on the left, the villages of Pofi and Arnara; with Castro, on the right, to Ceprano station (where we stop for lunch), on the Liris. A fine view can be had from the station of the valley of the Liris and Garigliano and the hills beyond, on which are the towns of Rocca d'Arce, S. Giovanni, Banco, Veroli, and Alatri. Opposite the station is the village of Falvaterra. All this beautiful country was devastated by Hannibal.

Proceeding, we cross the Liris, having Monte Opi on the left, and pass Isoletta station; then, on the right, S. Giovanni in Carico and Pico Farnese, to Roccasecca, to the left; Palazzuolo, Piedimonte, and Monte Cassino in the distance. We arrive at Aquino, on the right (the ancient Aquinum), birth-place of Juvenal, Pescennius Niger, and S. Thomas Aquinas.

"Farewell, then, and forget me not; and whenever Rome shall restore you to your native Aquinum, eager to refresh your strength, then you may tear me away too from Cumæ to Helvine Ceres, and your patron deity, Diana" (Juvenal, Sat. iii. 318).

Passing Pontecorvo, on the Liris, and winding round the base of Monte Cassino, past the ruins of the amphitheatre (erected by Numidia Quadratilla), we come to S. Germano, above which, on the top of a lofty hill, is the Monastery of Monte Cassino (Cassino station), belonging to the Benedictines, founded by S. Benedict in 529, on the site of the Temple of Apollo. It is an extensive establishment, and has a very imposing appearance. The church is one of the most highly decorated in Italy; and its library enjoys a world-wide celebrity. It well repays a visit. Varro had a villa here, which was the scene of some of the revellings of Mark Antony. (See Cicero, 2 Philippic, 40.)

Proceeding, we notice the fine view, and pass, on the left, Cervaro, S. Vittore, and S. Pietro in Fine; then Rocca d'Evandro and Gola di Mignano, on the right; entering the plain of the Volturno; Presenzano, on the left, to Caianiello Vairano, by Riardo; on the left, Teano; then Torre di Francolesi, on the right, to Sparanisi, where we get our first view of Vesuvius. A new line has been opened from here to Gaeta. Continuing our journey, we pass the ruined castle of Calvi and Pignataro station, where we enter the plain of Campagna Felice.

"The region of Campania is the finest of all countries, not only in Italy, but in the whole world. Nothing can be softer than its air: indeed, it produces flowers twice a year. Nothing can be more fertile than its soil, and it is therefore said to have been an object of contention between Ceres and Bacchus. Nothing can be more hospitable than its shores, for on them are those noble harbours Gaeta, Misenum, and Baiæ (with its warm springs), as well as the Lakes Lucrinus and Avernus (places of retirement, as it were, for the sea). Here, too, are those vine-clad mountains Gaurus, Falernus, Massicus, and Vesuvius (the finest of all, the imitator of the fires of Ætna). On the sea are the cities Formiæ, Cumæ, Puteoli, Naples, Herculaneum, Pompeii; and, the chief of all, Capua, which was formerly one of the three greatest cities of the world, Rome and Carthage being the others" (Florus, i. 16).

Crossing the Volturno, we stop under the walls of Capua. Two miles beyond is S. Maria, on the site of ancient Capua, now noted for the ruins of its amphitheatre, onwards to Caserta (*Casa-erta*, "the dreary house"), the junction for Benevento and Foggia. From Caserta a new line has been made by Cancello, Ottajano, and Torre Annunziata to Castellamare, thus avoiding Naples. On the left is the celebrated palace of Vanvitelli, belonging to the King of Italy, and well worth visiting. The front is 780 feet long, and 125 feet high, having thirty-seven windows on each story. On the right is a fine avenue.

We next pass Maddaloni station, with its medieval towers and castle, and the palace of the Carafas; Cancello, beyond, with a ruined castle, the junction for Nola, Codola, Avellino, and Benevento, and our last stoppage.

Proceeding through a fertile valley, we pass Acerra and Casalnuovo, by the Acqua di Carmignano, and canals of Regi Lagni. We obtain a fine view of Mount Vesuvius and the white walls of the Observatory half-way up, on our left; and the Castle of S. Elmo on the hills to the right. We run into the Naples station— we hope, after a pleasant journey.

OTHER RAILWAY ROUTES FROM NAPLES.

CENTRAL STATION.—Pompeii, Cava, Salerno, Battipagli, Potenza. Taranto, to Brindisi.
Portici, Torre del Greco, Annunziata, Castellamare, to Gragnano.
Poggioreale, Nola, to Bajano.
Caserta, Benevento, to Foggia and Brindisi.
Cancello, Nola, Avellino, to Benevento.
PIAZZA MUNICIPIO.—Ottajano and S. Giuseppe round the north side of Vesuvius.
PORTA CAPUA to Aversa.
PORTA CAPUA to Calvano.
MONTE SANTO.—Pozzuoli, Baiæ, and Torregaveta; hence steamers run to Procida and Ischia.
Funicular rail to the Vomero, close by S. Elmo.
CHIAIA.—Funicular rail by the Corso Vittorio Emanuele to the Vomero.

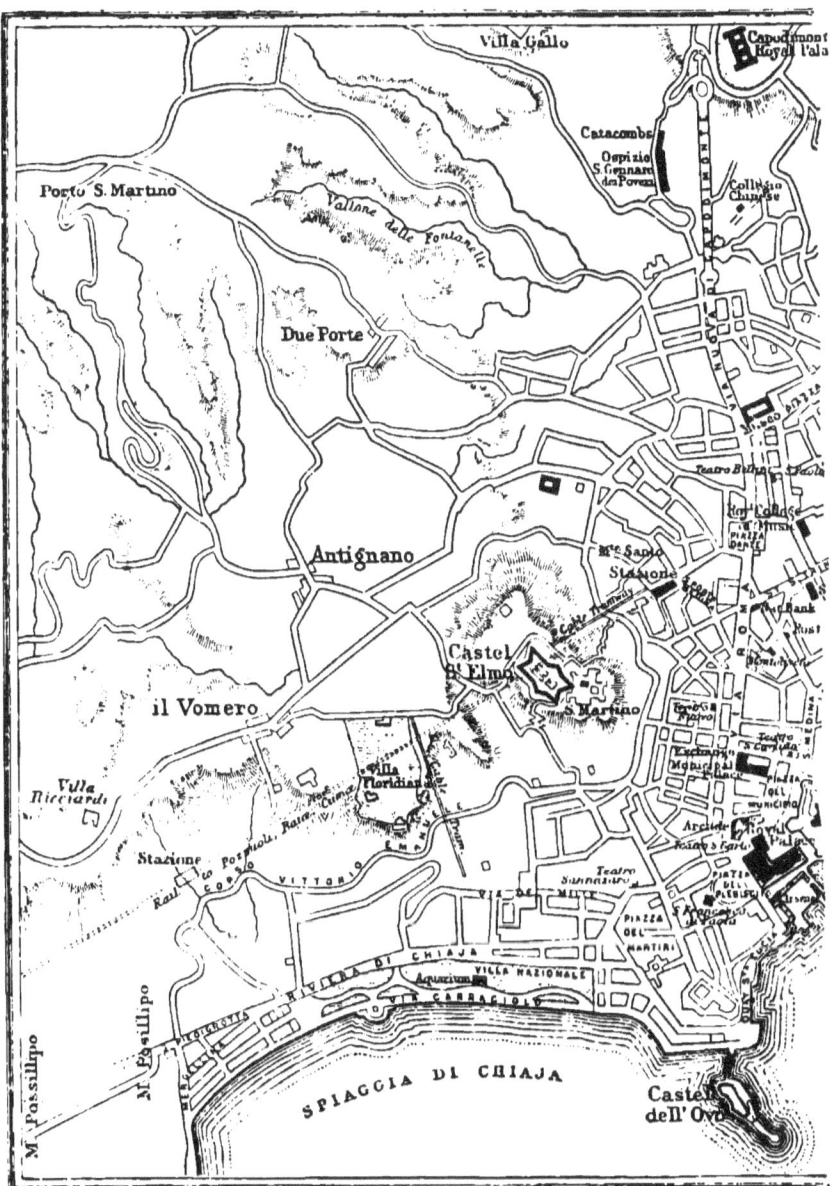

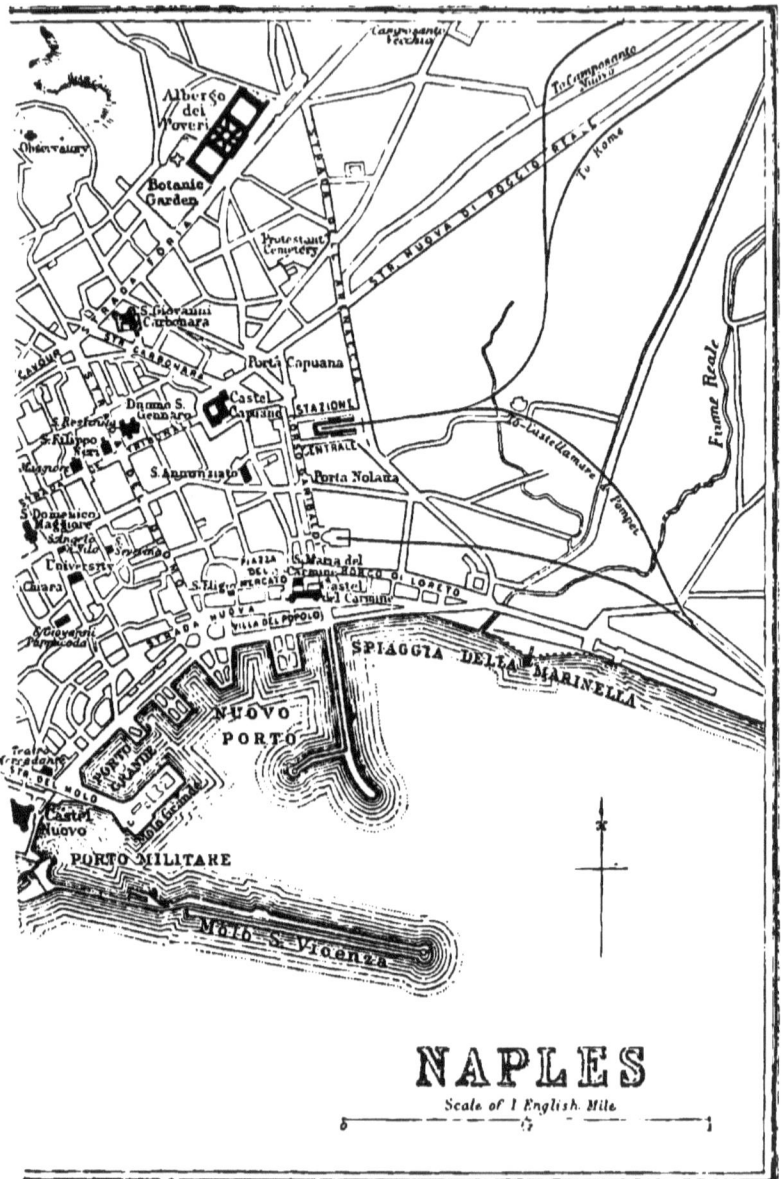

RAMBLES IN NAPLES.

RAMBLE I.

NAPLES—CASTELLO DELL' OVO—QUAY OF S. LUCIA—PIAZZA DEL PLEBISCITO—CHURCH OF S. FRANCESCO DI PAOLA—ROYAL PALACE—VIA ROMA—PIAZZA DANTE—NATIONAL MUSEUM—VILLA CAPODIMONTE—CHURCH OF S. GENNARO—CATACOMBS—GESÙ NUOVO—S. CHIARA—S. DOMENICO MAGGIORE—LA CAPPELLA DI S. SEVERO—S. ANNA DE' LOMBARDI—L'INCORONATA—PALAZZO FONDI—NEAPOLITAN LIFE

NAPLES.

"Vedi Napoli e poi mori!" (See Naples, and then die!) is the popular saying; but we would render it, "Before dying, see Naples!"

About one thousand years before Christ some Greek colonists from Cumæ founded a settlement which they named Parthenope, from the Siren's tomb (Pliny, iii. 9); these being augmented by fresh arrivals, enlarged their city, calling the old part Palæopolis, and the new part Neapolis. Both are now occupied by modern Naples. In A.U.C.* 535 they were taken by the Romans, and ever remained faithful, offering their treasure and arms against the Carthaginians (Livy, xxii. 32).

Scenery is the enchantment of Naples, which lies stretched out on a beautiful bay sloping down to the shore on the amphitheatre of the hills. Nothing in the world surpasses it, and it always exceeds the imagination. At the back of the city the peak of Capodimonte

* *Ab urbe condita* (From the building of the city Rome – B.C. 753).

rises and throws its spur towards the sea, S. Elmo occupying the centre and Pizzofalcone the shore, dividing the town into two unequal parts.

PIZZOFALCONE

was probably the site of the original settlement, and it was afterwards the site also of the Villa of Lucullus, where Romulus Augustulus, the last of the Roman emperors of the West, died in A.D. 476. It is now the barracks of the Bersaglieri.

THE ISLAND OF CASTELLO DELL' OVO

lies off the spur of S. Elmo called Pizzofalcone. It was the Megaris of Pliny (iii. 12). The castle, now a prison, was founded in 1154.

Following the road to the right (back to the sea) or east of the Pizzofalcone, we come to the

QUAY OF S. LUCIA,

ornamented with a fountain like a triumphal arch, with figures by Domenico d'Auria and Giovanni da Nola. It is the great resort of the Neapolitans upon *festas*, where their picturesque costumes may be studied. A drink can be had for 5 centesimi at the sulphur spring; and from the stalls *frutti di mare* can be eaten. Steamers leave here for Capri between 8 and 9 A.M.; office, A. Manzi & Co., Strada Pilioro. Tickets can be had at the landing-place. *The Strada del Gigante takes us into the*

PIAZZA DEL PLEBISCITO,

with its handsome colonnade. The municipality has erected a handsome fountain in the centre of the square in commemoration of the new water supply. The basin is 26 mètres in diameter, and holds 270 cubic mètres of water. A central jet throws water to the height of 45 mètres; this is surrounded by 380 minor jets, the whole throwing up 16,000 cubic mètres of water per day, equal to 32,000 bottles. On the right is the Prefettura, 31; on the left the house of the commandant, 27, where permissions are obtained to visit the Castle of S. Elmo. *In front is the*

CHURCH OF S. FRANCESCO DI PAOLA (11),

after the Pantheon at Rome. *Before it, on the right*, is a statue of Charles III.; *and on the left*, Ferdinand I. The church was erected in 1817-31, by the architect Bianchi di Lugano. The portico is formed with six Ionic columns, and the interior has thirty Corinthian columns from Mondragone. The high altar is beautifully inlaid with jasper and *lapis lazuli*, its side columns being of Egyptian breccia, very rare. *The opposite side of the square is occupied by the*

ROYAL PALACE,
(Palazzo Reale,)

designed by Fontana, the Roman architect. The façade is 185 yards in length, and is three stories high. In the small enclosed garden in front is the statue of Italia.

Apply to the porter for permissions to visit the royal villas and palaces. Porter's fee, 50 centesimi; attendant's fee, 1 lira.

A grand staircase leads into the upper or royal apartments. It is formed of white marble, and is decorated with reliefs and statues, the rivers Ebro and Tagus occupying the foot. The rooms contain modern works of art and porcelain. In one room is a fine tapestry of the death of Admiral Coligny: his mute appeal is striking. From the garden terrace a fine view can be had of the Bay of Naples, looking seaward.

Crossing the Piazza S. Ferdinando, the starting-place of the omnibuses and tramways, we reach the

VIA ROMA,
(formerly Toledo,)

the principal business street of Naples, and intersecting the city from south to north. At the Piazza della Carità, opposite the statue of Carlo Poerio, Strada Nuova Monteoliveto, a street on the right leads into the Piazza Monteoliveto, where are the General Post and Telegraph Office, 62. To the left is the Monte Santo station for Pozzuoli, Baiæ, Cumæ. *Continuing up the Via Roma, we reach the*

PIAZZA DANTE,

with Dante's monument, by Angelini and Solari, erected in 1872. *Beyond* is the circular entrance of the Liceo Ginnasiale Vittorio Emanuele or Circus. Its front is decorated with twenty-six statues, erected in 1857, by Naples, in honour of Charles III.: they represent his virtues. *To the left* is the Porta Alba, one of the medieval city gates, with its bronze statue of S. Gætano, erected in 1632.

Just beyond, on the right, is the

GALLERIA PRINCIPE DI NAPOLI,

a very handsome modern building, in which there are some very good shops, as in our arcades. The Caffè Restaurant Santangelo is a good place to lunch after seeing the Museum.

The next block, also on the right, is the

NAPLES NATIONAL MUSEUM,

(*Museo Nazionale,*)

Open (from November 1st to April 30th) from 10 A.M. till 4 P.M.; from May 1st to October 31st, from 9 A.M. till 3 P.M. Entrance fee, 1 lira; children, half-price. Sundays, free.

Visitors will find it advantageous to visit the Museum at Naples before seeing Pompeii. They will appreciate the ruins more by seeing first the objects they contained. It will require several visits to exhaust this valuable collection. We would advise at least two visits for the antiquities and another for the pictures.

We here mention the principal objects. We do not hold ourselves responsible for changes that may be made in the numbers. This is so often done that we think it must be for the amusement of the guardians. They are now adopting the capital plan of placing the names on the subjects, which might be followed in other museums.

THE GRAND VESTIBULE.

In entering (*right*), Alexander Severus; (*left*) Melpomene. From Pompey's Theatre. At the foot of the stairs two river gods. *Right*, Flora; *left*, Genius of the Roman army.

HALLS OF FRESCOES.

Door immediately to right on entering Vestibule. We have here the most valuable of the wall paintings of ancient art from Pompeii and Herculaneum, representing mural decorations and mythological scenes; occupying seven rooms and corridors. The second panel on the left is from the Temple of Isis, representing Roman galleys in full chase.

Entering the main halls, we take the subjects on our right, and work round the compartments till we gain the door again, the subjects being always on our right.

8940. Victory. 8946. A good half-figure of Psyche. 9110. Achilles recognized by Ulysses amongst the maids of the Court of Lycomedes, with whom he had hid to escape going to the siege of Troy. The same subject is represented on the sarcophagus in the Capitoline Museum. 9109. Charon and Achilles. 9105. The heralds of Agamemnon demanding Briseis of Achilles: Patroclus is leading Briseis to the audience. From house of the tragic poet. 9088. A girl arranging her hair. 9097. A girl in meditation. 9058. Paquius Proculus and his wife. Proculus was a baker, and chief magistrate of

PLAN OF GROUND FLOOR OF NATIONAL MUSEUM

Pompeii. 9059-71 represent scenes in the Forum at Pompeii. In 9066 a boy is being "hoisted." 9043 and 9049. Scenes from the story of Theseus. *We next enter the compartment of the*

MOSAICS.

In the centre is a mosaic representing Love's conquest over Strength. On the right, 10018, 10014, 10012. Wall decorations. 12284. Black and white mosaic, representing the sea-gate at Pompeii, with a vessel in port. 10004. The three Graces. 10007. The marriage of Neptune and Amphitrite. 9037. "Cave canem."
10002. "Cave canem" (Beware of the dog). From the house of the tragic poet.

CAVE CANEM.

"But while I was staring open-mouthed at all I saw before, I had liked to have fallen backwards and broken my legs. For to the left, as we entered, not far from the porter's lodge, an enormous chained dog was painted on the wall, with an inscription over it in capital letters: BEWARE OF THE DOG" (Petronius Arbiter, v.).
10003. Dwarf feeding two game-cocks. Two columns in mosaic. 9997. Fish. The various kinds still taken in the Bay of Naples are here represented. In the centre is a fight between a crawfish and an octopus. The border of foliage, flowers, cupids, birds, and snails is very beautiful. 9998, 9999. Sea-bird. Columns of mosaic and shells. 9993. Cat attacking a chicken. 9991. The genius of Bacchus mounted on a panther. 9992. Parrots pluming themselves in a basin of water, watched by a cat,—a companion mosaic to the celebrated Pliny's doves in the Capitol. 9994. Wreath of leaves, flowers, and fruit. *Window.* 9990 (*below*). An allegorical representation of the Nile. 9978. A skeleton in mosaic, with a vase in each hand. Used to remind banqueters of the future. "In came a servant with a silver skeleton, so artfully put together that its joints and backbone turned every way. Having cast it a few times on the table, and made it assume various postures, Trimalchio cried out,—

' Vain as vanity are we,
Life's swift transient flames decay!
What this is we soon shall be;
Then be merry whilst you may.' "

PETRONIUS ARBITER, V.

It was an Egyptian custom (Herodotus, ii. 78; Plutarch, in "Conviv. Sapientes," vi.). 109982. Ancient Masonic mosaic. During the explorations of Pompeii in the year 1874 there was found a most beautiful piece of mosaic work, which, from its wonderful and unique formation and workmanship, has caused much excitement. It is a mosaic table of square shape, and little more than a foot square, fixed in a strong wooden frame, and has been placed in the National Museum at Naples. It served as the top of the pedestal in the Masonic lodge at Pompeii. The ground is of a gray-green stone, in the middle of which is a human skull, made of white, gray, and black colours. In appearance the skull is quite natural, and the beauty of its execution is such as to render it a model of anatomical precision and truthfulness. The eyes, nostrils, teeth, ears, and coronal are all well executed. Above the skull is seen a level of coloured wood, the points being of brass; and from the top point, by a white thread, is suspended a plumb-line. Below the skull is a wheel with six spokes, and on the upper rim of the wheel there is a butterfly, with wings of a red colour, edged with yellow; the eyes are of blue. The outline of the entire piece is symmetrical, so that the skull, wings, and wheel, through the protraction of the plumb-lines, become halved. Looking sideways, the objects correspond with each other. On the left is an upright spear, the bottom of which is of iron, resting on the ground; from this there hangs, attached to a golden cord, a garment of scarlet, also a purple robe, to which some signification may be surmised; whilst the upper part of the spear is surrounded by a white braid of diamond pattern. To the right is a gnarled thorn stick, from which hangs a coarse, shaggy piece of cloth in yellow, gray, and brown colours, which is tied with a ribbon; and above it is a leathern knapsack. Evidently this work of art, by its composition, is mystical and symbolical; at all events, it appears to have some reference to the royal craft, and as a proof of this last supposition it certainly has reference to some secret craft in the old Roman era. The antiquity of the origin of the K.K. (king's kraft, royal craft), and of the brotherhood, and its fellowship with ancient seerecy and mysteries, becomes at last certified by this wondrous piece of mosaic art, as acknowledged by affirmed known facts. 9986. A greenroom. 9985. Actors: made by Dioskorides of Samos. 9987 is a companion.

Re-entering the
HALLS OF FRESCOES.

9010. The entry of the wooden horse into Troy. 9008. Story of the hind feeding Telephus. 8997, 8998. Perseus showing the head of Medusa, reflected in a brook, to Andromeda. 8991. Dædalus murdering his nephew Perdix, the inventor of the saw, chisel, compass, and potter's wheel. 8980. Atalanta and Meleager. 8976. Medea. 9111. Orestes and Pylades. 9112. Diana saves Iphigenia from death by substituting a stag at the moment of sacrifice. This was probably a copy of the celebrated painting by the Greek artist Timanthes mentioned by Pliny (xxxv. 36): "As to Timanthes, he was an artist highly gifted with genius, and loud have some of the orators been in their commendations of his Iphigenia, represented as she stands at the altar awaiting her doom. Upon the countenances of all present, that of her uncle in particular, grief was depicted; but having already exhausted all the characteristic features of sorrow, the artist adopted the device of veiling the features of the victim's father, Agamemnon, finding himself unable adequately to give expression to his feelings." Our thoughts naturally turn to the story of Abraham and Isaac in beholding this picture. *Under the window* are two cases containing ancient colours found at Pompeii. 8905. The worship of Ceres. 8898. Europe, Asia, and Africa. 8895. A fine head, crowned with a wreath. 8959. A sea-monster carrying off a Nereid : reminding us of the sculpture after Scopas, in the Vatican. 9118, 9119, 9121. Fauns dancing on the tight-rope. 8852-8855. Tritons. 9292, 9295, 9297, 9299. Bacchantes. 9278. Ariadne and Bacchus. 9256, 9257. Cupid, Venus, and Urania. 9248, 9249. Venus and Mars. 9301. Diana. 9560-9564, 109370. Six outline-paintings, in one colour, on marble, called monocromes ; unique. Painted by Alexander of Athens. 9558, 9559. Story of Io, Juno, and Jupiter. 9539, 9538. Apollo and Marsyas. 9519-9521. The days of the week. *Compartments LXVII., LXVI., LXV.* Landscapes. 9453-9457. Worship of Ceres. *Compartments LXI., LXII., LXIII.* Landscapes. 9364-9351. Etruscan frescoes. *Compartment LVII.* Cupids. 9236, 9231. The three Graces. 9202. Flora, Cupids, and Zephyrus. 9194. Two Cupids raising a May-pole; another holds up a cross towards them. 9169, 9164. Seated Psyches and Cupids. 9180. Woman selling Cupids. 9181. Head of Venus. 8819. Apollo.

We here re-enter the Corridor of Frescoes, and turn to the left, into the

CORRIDOR OF INSCRIPTIONS.

On the right, half-way down, are the statues of Tiberius and Neoptolemus.

Between them we enter the

GALLERY OF INSCRIPTIONS.

To the right, the Farnese Hercules leaning on his club, the work of Gycon of Athens: from the Baths of Caracalla. *To the left*, the Farnese Bull, by Apollonius and Thauriscus of Rhodes; one of the finest groups of ancient art: from the Baths of Caracalla.

Pliny (xxxvi. 4) says: "Zethus and Amphion, with Dirce, the bull, and the halter, all sculptured from a single block of marble, the work of Apollonius and Thauriscus, and brought to Rome from Rhodes." Zethus and Amphion bound Dirce, queen of Thebes, to a wild bull, in revenge for the death of their mother, who had been so treated by Dirce.

Returning into the corridor, off it, on the left, is a room containing medieval works; amongst others, The Modesty, by Sammartino.

A broad marble staircase leads to the basement, containing

EGYPTIAN ANTIQUITIES,

where is the statue of Jupiter Serapis found at Pozzuoli, Christian inscriptions, mummies, and Egyptian gods. 976. Statue of Isis, from temple at Pompeii.

Ascending, passing out of the gallery, turn right, then left, through

CORRIDORS OF STUCCO AND FRESCOES

from Pompeii, mostly mural decorations. A niche on the right contains a frescoed pier representing the fuller's art.

Crossing the grand vestibule, we enter the

CORRIDOR OF SCULPTURES.

6006. Electra urging Orestes to avenge the murder of their father Agamemnon. 6007. An archaic statue of Pallas with the ægis. 6009-10. Harmodius and Aristogiton, who delivered Athens from the Pisistratidæ by killing Hipparchus, 514 B.C. 6011. A copy of the Doryphorus, by Polycletus. 6017. A very beautiful statue called the Venus of Capua. The arms are restored. This is not a Venus, but Victory, and is similar to the Nike of the Louvre, the so-called Venus de Melos. She should hold a shield in her hands, like the Victory at Brescia. We believe this is the statue of Victory spoken of by Cicero ("Divi." i. 43) as on a certain occasion being "covered with a miraculous sweat." 6020. Venus Callipygos (so called from that part of her body at which she is looking), from the Baths of Caracalla. 6012-15. Reclining—an Amazon, a Persian, a

Gaul (like the dying Gaul of the Capitol). 6023. Bust of Homer. 6028. Bust of Pompey the Great. *In the recess* a porphyry vase from Caracalla's Baths. 6224. A fragment representing the head and shoulders of the father in the Laocoon group of the Vatican, showing how erroneous are the restorations there made by Bernini and Cornacchini. The right hand is behind the head. 6025. Brutus's bust. 6022. Silenus carrying the infant Bacchus—the Faun's head does not belong to it. 6026. A Nereid on a sea-monster. 6027. Juno. 6029. The younger Agrippina, mother of Nero, similar to the one of the elder Agrippina in the Capitol. 6034. Torso of Bacchus, a very fine fragment. 6019. Psyche, from Capua, a beautiful Greek ideal personification of the soul, *the Ione of Bulwer.* 6030. Antinous, Hadrian's ideal of self-sacrifice. *Turn to the left in going up the*

CORRIDOR OF STATUES.

6211. Equestrian statue of Marcus Nonius Balbus, the elder, from Herculaneum. Head modern. 6167. A statue of the same. 6168. Viciria Archas, the mother of Balbus. 6235. Suedius Clemens. 6233. Marcus Holconius Rufus. On the plinth is inscribed—"To Marcus Holconius Rufus, son of Marcus, a duumvir and mayor for the fifth time, quinquennalis for the second time, elected by the people military tribune, a priest of Augustus, patron of the colony (of Pompeii)." 6119. A hunter. 6107. A priestess. *Turn up the corridor.* 6136. Bust of Lycurgus, who lost his left eye in a riot at Sparta. He was the famous Spartan legislator, 800 B.C. 6137. Hannibal. This was found at Capua. Its authenticity is doubtful. 6146. Herodotus, the father of history, 450 B.C. 6104. Equestrian statue of the younger Marcus Nonius Balbus, very fine. 6188. A vestal. 6189. Cleopatra (?). 6232. To Eumachia, daughter of Lucius, public priestess, this statue was dedicated by the fullers. From their hall at Pompeii. 6177. Cicero. 6179. Lucius Junius Brutus. 6210. Valerius Publicola. 6212. A hired mourner. 6118. A pig in a caldron, with two men scraping it. *Turn to the left into the*

HALL OF VASES AND CANDELABRA.

6788-6791. Beautiful door ornaments from Pompeii. 6857. Tasteful candelabrum. 6862. Rosso antico vase.

HALL OF RELIEFS.

Left:—6753, 6757, 6763. Reliefs, figures representing provinces, found in the Piazza di Pietra, Rome, and companions to those in the

Court of the Palazzo dei Conservatori of the Capitol. 6738, 6739 (*above*). Trophies belonging to the provinces. 6776. Sarcophagus : the Triumph of Bacchus. 6678. A sacrifice vowed for the safety and victory of Marcus Aurelius. 6679. Initiation into the Bacchanal rites. 6682. Temptation of Helen. 6684. A drunken Bacchus supported by a faun. 6685. Silenus drunk, riding upon an ass. 6687. Comic scene. 6688. Apollo and the three Graces. 6690. Woman and bird. 6691. Tiberius and his wife on a horse. 6693. Sarcophagus : Bacchus and Silenus. 6704. Relief : Life of a Gladiator. 6705. Sarcophagus : Creation of Man, by Prometheus. 6715. Two beautiful Caryatides, with a female seated under a tree, with inscription : "Greece erected this trophy after their victory over the Caryans, who had gone over to the Persians." 6725. Relief : Euphrosyne, Aglaia, and Thalia, the three Graces, hand in hand with Ismene, Hikasis, Eranno, and Telonnesos. 6727. Orpheus, Eurydice, and Mercury. 6728. Bacchus presenting the *cantharus* to another figure, effaced. 6780 (*in the centre of the hall*). A pedestal bears the personification of fourteen cities of Asia Minor, rebuilt by Tiberius after an earthquake. They were eased of tribute for three years (Tacitus, "Ann." iv. 13).

HALL OF MASKS.

On the left is a case with statuettes and double Hermes busts. 6671. Well-head sculptured with vines. 6556. Archaic, man and dog. 6672. A table-foot representing a Centaur, Cupid, and Scylla. 6600, 6601. Galleys. 6003. A marriage. 6673 (*in the centre of the hall*). The Gaeta Vase, by Salpion the Athenian : Mercury presenting the infant Bacchus to the nymph Nisa.

HALL OF FLORA.

On the pavement, a beautiful mosaic from the house of the Faun at Pompeii, representing the battle of Issus, between Darius and Alexander the Great. *Left :*—6411. Protesilaus. 6416. The Wounded Gladiator. He has received his death-wound in the region of the heart, and is staggering towards the spectators. 6408. A gladiator. 6409. Flora, by Praxiteles. The form is beautifully shown through her flowing robes From the Baths of Caracalla. 6410. A gladiator.

HALL OF THE MUSES.

6405. Wounded amazon on horseback. 6406. Hercules and Omphale. Love conquers strength. 6407. Warrior on horseback.

6401. Clio, muse of history. 6404. Polyhymnia, sacred song, muse of memory and eloquence. 6402. Erato, of love poetry. 6400. Melpomene, of tragedy. 6399. Thalia, of comedy. 6395. Euterpe, of music. 6377. Calliope, of heroic poetry. 6376. Urania, of astronomy. 6378. Mnemosyne, their mother.

HALL OF ATLAS.

6358. Paris, with a dog. 6365. Naiad seated on a rock. 6329. Marsyas and Olympus. 6331. Satyr with grapes. 6334. Kneeling satyr. 6339. Sleeping Cupid. 6351 - 6355. Ganymede and the eagle. 6353. Cupid, like that of the Vatican ; a copy of the original by Praxiteles. *Centre of hall:*—6374. Atlas supporting the celestial globe, showing forty-two constellations. 6375. Cupid and dolphin.

HALL OF VENUS.

6323 (*in centre of room*). Mars seated. 6307. Bacchus and Acratus. 6311. Bacchus and a panther. 6314. Antinous as Bacchus. 6321. Minerva. 6283. Venus crouching with a Cupid. 6297. Seated Venus. 6301, 109608. Venus painted. (It is not a new fashion for ladies to paint.)

HALL OF APOLLO.

In the centre, a colossal porphyry statue of Apollo, with Luna marble extremities. 6278. Diana of Ephesus, composed of alabaster and bronze. This gives us a good idea of the "great Diana of the Ephesians," and of the small statuettes made by Demetrius (Acts xix.). 6262. Apollo, the leader of the Muses, in basalt. 6273. Ceres. 6274. Jupiter Ammon.

We here cross the CORRIDOR OF STATUES (*left:*—6118. A kneeling Phrygian in coloured marble. *Right:*—6117. Fifteen Phrygians in pavonazzeto marble), *and enter*

FIRST BRONZE HALL.

4877. Colossal horse's head, the old coat of arms of Naples. 4888. Six gazelles. 4892. Mercury seated. 4895. Diana, with enamel eyes, used as an oracle. See hole in back of the head. Glass case with small objects. *Notice* two bronze wings. 4904. A horse from Herculaneum, one of four that surmounted Nero's Arch.

SECOND HALL.

Round the room are cases with small objects. *Centre:-* 111697. Abundance, seated. 111170. Cupid carrying a dolphin, which served as a fountain. 5000. Boy and goose. "Boethus [of Carthage], although more celebrated for his works in silver, has executed a beautiful figure of a child strangling a goose" (Pliny, xxxiv. 19). There is a marble copy in the Capitoline Museum. 4995. Bacchus and Ampelus. 4999. An amazon. 4996. Alexander the Great. 4997. Victory. 5003. Narcissus, exquisite. 111495. A charming bronze faun, a statuette, and the ornament of a fountain ; in execution, dimensions, and type, forms one of the group of the celebrated Narcissus, dancing faun, and Silenus. The eye is at once attracted by the bold, free, and graceful attitude of this figure, the muscular yet elegant proportions of which an unusually thick earthy incrustation, chemically united with the oxide, in vain tries to hide. The faun leans far back ; the weight of the body rests on the right leg, the left being extended forward to preserve the balance. The wine-skin is squeezed under and held by the left arm, the hand of which grasps the spigot. The right arm and hand are lowered and slightly drawn back, in the attitude of one holding a cup to receive the stream of wine. A tube at the back of the figure led the water into the wine-skin, from whence it issued from the spigot. The shape of the head is very beautiful ; the locks of hair falling over the brow are admirably indicated ; a wreath (probably a vine branch with grapes) crowns the head, but is made indistinct by the incrustations. The ears are pointed, and there is the usual tail. The face and figure express that joyous abandonment of a youthful votary of Bacchus. The house in which it was found is called Casa del Centenario. 5002. Dancing faun, which gave its name to the house at Pompeii. 5001. Silenus.

THIRD HALL.

Left:—5619-5621. Dancers. 5589. Ciria, mother of Balbus. 5591. Lucius Mammius Matimus Augustalis, the inhabitants contributing the money. 5593. Tiberius Claudius Drusus. 5595. Augustus, deified. 5597. Marcus Calatorus. 5603-5605. Actresses. 5611. A Camillus. 5612. Faustina. 5615. Nero. 5616. Seneca. *In the centre:*—5624. Faun asleep. 5626. Discobolus. 5629. Apollo discharging an arrow. 5630. Apollo. 5627. Discobolus. 5628. Drunken faun. 5625. Mercury in repose.

FOURTH ROOM.

Equestrian bronze statue of Nero, similar to that of M. Aurelius on the Capitol. Greek, Roman, and gladiatorial armour in cases. 5634. Scipio Africanus.

Returning through the Bronze Rooms, turn to the right, then to the right again; we enter the

HALL OF EMPERORS AND THEIR WIVES.

As all these statues have their names on metal plates, it is unnecessary for us to enumerate them. There are none of them that call for any special mention, after seeing those in the museums at Rome.

We now ascend the stairs at the end of the vestibule to the

ENTRESOL, OR MEZZANINO.

Left. CUMÆAN COLLECTION. — *First Hall.* Arranged in cases: vases, cups, glass bottles and plates, beads, amphoræ, Italo-Greek vases, etc. *Second Hall.* A wax mask found in a tomb; jewellery; a vase representing combats between the Amazons and Greeks, with their names; glass and terra-cotta vases sculptured. For the models of the temples see page 132.

Right. ROOM OF FRESCOES.—111475. Capture of Europa. 113197. Found at Pompeii in June 1882, and highly interesting from the subject represented,—The Judgment of Solomon (1 Kings iii. 16-28). The scene illustrates verse 26: "O my lord, give her the living child, and in no wise slay it." "Until very recently there has never been, in Pompeii or Herculaneum, the slightest trace of any idea referable to a Jewish or Christian source. But in the progress of excavations, which have been of late diligently and carefully renewed by the government, a striking discovery has been made of a character thought by many to be clearly exceptional in this particular. A few years ago there was removed from Pompeii to the Naples museum, where it was placed among the Pompeian frescoes, a picture, 5½ feet in length by 1 foot 7 inches in height, which in the opinion of many good critics stands for the judgment of Solomon. The scene is laid on a terrace in front of a house, which is shaded with a white awning and festooned with creeping plants. On a platform, which would be about four feet in height, sits the king, holding a sceptre and robed in white; on each side a counsellor, with six armed men in the rear. The king leans over the front of the platform towards a woman in a green robe, who is kneeling before him with outstretched hand and dishevelled hair. In the centre of the foreground is a three-legged table, on which lies an infant, held down, in spite of its struggles, by a woman wearing a turban. An armour-clad soldier, having on his head a helmet with a long red plume, holds the child's legs, and is about to cleave it in twain with his falchion. The colouring of this early specimen of mural art is particularly bright and fresh. The drawing is inartistic, yet full of spirit and expression. The artist, apparently in his anxiety to develop strongly the expression of the faces of the figures, has exaggerated the heads in size and rather dwarfed the bodies. At first glance this might suggest caricature, but the marked agony of the kneeling mother, the absorbed attention of the listening king, the complacency of the second woman, who appears to be gloating over the fate threatened by the lifted weapon, appear to repel all idea of travesty. No other discoveries were made in the exhumation of the house from which this was taken which would tend to shed light upon its occupant's faith, or confirm the suspicion that some Jew had made his home even there. But if this be indeed the first hint looking in that direction, it surely deserves remembrance. Anyhow, the stones of the desert, the mounds of the plains, and the exhumed frescoes of early art, all combine to bear testimony to the truth of the Divine Word" (*Homiletic Magazine*). 111441. Cupid urging the suit of Orion to Diana. 111436. An ox about to be sacrificed, calling to our minds the scene at Lystra, when the people took Barnabas for Jupiter and Paul for Mercury : "Then the priest of Jupiter, which was before their city, brought oxen and garlands unto the gates, and would have done sacrifice with the people" (Acts xiv. 13). 112285. The guardians of the Lares attacking a man, above whom is written, "Cacator cave malum." Fortune stands on the right. 111479. The destruction of the children of Niobe. 112222 The Amphitheatre of Pompeii is here depicted, illustrating the scene as described by Tacitus, "Ann." xiv. 17, A.D. 59. (See page 64.) The awning is depicted as rolled up, not spread, and the *spoliarium* is shown to our right of the Amphitheatre. In the foreground, under the trees, refreshments are sold. 111473. Pan and nymphs, with farm in the background. The case in the centre is for Pompeian terra-cottas.

SECOND ROOM.—Frescoes lately found at Pompeii. Two heads crowned with bay, and with rolls in their hands. On one is written Homer, and on the other Sappho. They are imaginary portraits.

THIRD ROOM.—Ancient glass in cases. *Centre:*—13688. A *patera* in blue glass, with white handles. 13522. A blue glass plate inlaid with gold. 13521. Blue glass amphora upon a modern silver stand, found filled with ashes in a tomb at Pompeii, representing the genii of the vintage as on the sarcophagus of Constantina in the Vatican, and the mosaic work on her tomb near Rome.

FOURTH, FIFTH, AND SIXTH ROOMS.—Glass and terra-cotta used for domestic purposes. In the Fifth Room, 1041, are the Volscian reliefs found at Velletri in 1784.

Ascending the stair to the upper floor, the door on the left leads to

THE NUMISMATIC COLLECTION,

consisting of 50,000 specimens in the history of Italy, arranged in six halls, having ancient mosaic pavements and maps upon the walls; also a numismatic library. The compartments are arranged in the following order: Greek, Roman, Medieval, Modern, Dies of the old Naples Mint. Professor Fiorelli has prepared an excellent catalogue, which hangs above each case.

Opposite is the

CABINET OGGETTI OSCENI,

consisting of frescoes, bronzes, and silver, not of much account. *Gentlemen only admitted.*

THE PICTURE GALLERY

in this wing is arranged in rooms according to schools, in the following order: Bolognese, Tuscan, Neapolitan, German, Dutch.

There are catalogues fixed at the doors of each room, but as they are rather awkward to consult, we call attention to the principal masterpieces.

BOLOGNESE SCHOOL.—1. Woman of Samaria, by Lavinia Fontana. 3. Virgin and Child; *reverse*, Annunciation, by A. Caracci, on a piece of agate. 7. Infant Jesus Asleep, by Guido Reni. 11. S. John, after Domenichino. 17. Flight into Egypt, same. 21. Timoclea thrusting a Captain into a Well, who hoped to find Treasure by descending, by Elizabeth Sirani, 1600 A.D. 25. Apollo in Space, by A. Caracci. 36. Hercules between Virtue and Vice, same. 38. Sibyl, by Romanelli. 44. Modesty and Vanity, by Guido Reni. 52. Madonna, Jesus, and John, by Raibolino. 65. Angels with Censers, by A. Caracci. 69. Judith slaying Holofernes, by Caravaggio. 70. The Virgin giving Jesus to S. Pasquale, by Guercino. 72. Martyrdom of SS. Philip and James, by D. Muratori; sketch of the fresco in SS. Apostoli, Rome.

TUSCAN SCHOOL.—*Centre.* Bronze Tabernacle, by Jacopo Siciliani, a pupil of Michael Angelo. 2. Holy Family, by Jacopo Carduzzi; a copy of original, by Andrea del Sarto. 4. Marriage of Mary and

Joseph, by Cosimo Rosselli. 6. Holy Family, by Bronzino (Angelo Allori). 24. Mary and Jesus Enthroned, by Jacopo Pacchiarotti. 30. Virgin and Christ, by Ghirlandaio. 32. Virgin and Jesus, by Sandro Botticelli. 33. Mary, Jesus, and John, by A. Pollaiuolo. 36. Ecce Homo, by Bronzino. 37. Annunciation, by Filippo Lippi. 44. His Portrait, by Masaccio.

NEAPOLITAN SCHOOL.—1. Crucifixion, by Pietro del Donzello. 7. Madonna and Christ with Saints, by Antonio Solari (Il Zingaro). 27. S. James of Galitz charging the Saracens, by Belisario Corenzio. 34. Adoration of the Magi, by Andrea da Salerno.

In adjoining room are specimens of the Byzantine and early Tuscan Schools.

Room beyond.—Neapolitan Schools of the thirteenth and fourteenth centuries very much restored.

LATER NEAPOLITAN SCHOOL.—13. Mary and Joseph with the Sleeping Jesus, by Gennaro Sarnelli. 18. Charitas (S. Francis of Paola), school of Giordano. 24. Adoration of the Shepherds, by Paolo de Matteis. 59. Parable of the Mote and the Beam, by Salvator Rosa. 61. Marriage at Cana, by Giordano. 69. Salome with the Head of John, by Giordano. 71. Madonna and Saints, same. 72. Masaniello, by Spadaro. 95. S. Agatha, school of Stanzioni. 96. The Virgin in Priest's Robes, by B. Rodgerio. 100. Jesus and S. Antony, by Vaccaro.

In the centre of this hall is a beautiful cabinet of walnut, from the Vestry S. Agostino degli Scalzi, made by one of the brothers in the sixteenth century, upon which are carved the life of S. Austin and numerous Cupids. It contains fifteenth century works of art in ivory, rock-crystal, ebony, glass, the sword of Alexander Farnese, mosaics, amber box, onyx vase, fans.

Another cabinet, formerly the door of the vestry, contains a collection of Abruzzi and Urbino ware; the Farnese Casket, said to be the work of Benvenuto Cellini, representing a temple.

GERMAN AND DUTCH SCHOOLS.—3. Adoration of the Magi, by L. Damnez (Luca d'Olanda). 11. Festival at Rotterdam, by J. Bruegel. 31. Triptych of the Nativity, by Van Orley. 42. François, Husband of Mary, Queen of Scots (1558 A.D.), by C. Amberger. 44. S. Jerome and the Lion, by Jan Van Eyck. 50. A Thief (the World) Stealing the Purse of a Monk, by Bruegel, 1565 A.D.

FLEMISH SCHOOL.—4. Violin-player, by Teniers, jun. 17. Rembrandt's Portrait, by himself. 32. Battle, by Wouwermans. 56. Skaters, by Wilhelm Schellings. 81. A Tavern, by Teniers, sen.

HALLS OF ITALO-GREEK VASES.

Entered from seventh Picture Room, containing over three thousand specimens of terra-cotta, arranged in seven rooms, with mosaic pavements from Pompeii. 2107, in the second room, *right*, represents a man riding on a bicycle. In the end room is a model tomb to show how the vases were placed.

From the first of these rooms we enter, on the left, the

SANTANGELO COLLECTION,

composed of vases, glass, mosaics, terra-cottas, and coins, purchased by the Naples Municipality in 1865 for 215,000 lire. There is a valuable collection of over 12,000 Greek coins. The mosaic pavements are from Pompeii.

From the eighth Picture Room we enter the

HALLS OF SMALL BRONZES,

consisting of ancient bronze domestic utensils found at Pompeii and Herculaneum, arranged in two rooms. Here may be seen kitchen utensils, weights, scales, lamps, stoves, iron bedsteads, surgical and musical instruments, chairs, water-cocks and taps, arms and toilet articles, sacrificial vases, dishes, urns, agricultural tools, and many things similar to those in use at the present day—showing that the ancients knew far more than they generally get credit for.

FIRST ROOM.—72983 (*at the corner of the objects placed in the centre*). A kitchener, in the shape of a fortress, adapted for every cooking purpose, and to warm the room. *Right:*—72985. A triclinium, or banqueting-couch. 73018. Cylindrical stove and boiler. 72984. A brazier. 72987. A beautiful pedestal for a table, with an exquisite Victory in front. 72988. Bisellium or chair of state. There are others similar in this room. 72995. Tripod for sacrifices, from Herculaneum, of the finest workmanship. 72998. Stocks from Pompeii, such as Paul and Silas were put into. The jailer "thrust them into the inner prison, and made their feet fast in the stocks" (Acts xvi. 24). 109697. A graceful vase. The handles are very beautifully formed with acanthus leaves, out of which peeps the head of Medusa. 73000. Candelabrum, formed with a square fluted pilaster supporting a Corinthian capital. 73003. Seven baths. 73005. Brazier from the baths at Pompeii. In the centre are three iron safes. Many curious specimens of small objects may be observed in the cases round the room.

SECOND ROOM.—In the centre is an interesting model of the city of Pompeii, where its topography can be conveniently studied and its position and buildings taken in a bird's-eye view. The model is made of cork, and added to as the excavations progress. The scale is 1 to 100. There is also a model of the house of the tragic poet. In the case at the end of the room, in entering on the left, 73880, is an urn for heating wine, similar to a tea-urn or samovar. 111048. Urn: *notice*, Cupid striding a Dolphin forms the tap. 78614 (*at end of room*). Bedsteads: the red painted wood is a restoration. 78673. Brazier, on the principle of the tubular boiler. In the cases round the room are musical instruments, toys, dice, theatrical tickets, toilet requisites, sculptors' tools, fishing-tackle, weights, writing materials, and surgical instruments. For these latter, see Table lxv., No. 77982, and following.

A discovery has lately been made in Pompeii which is well worth noting, in the shape of a quadrivalve speculum of great beauty, and in a high state of preservation. By competent persons who have examined it, the mechanism of it is said to be very ingenious. In the museum there are now three Pompeian specula—one a bivalve, one a trivalve, and the one just found a quadrivalve. This last is of a construction so uniform and well-proportioned, admitting the expansion of the valves, as to be superior to many of modern construction. It is noted as a curious fact that in its various dimensions it observes constantly the centimetric measurement. It will be found, in fact, on inspecting the cases round these rooms, that many of the instruments believed to be of modern invention are clearly only exhumations of the past.

Beyond is the

CABINET OF GEMS,

containing 2,000 specimens of cameos, intaglios, gold and silver; also the celebrated Tazze Farnese, an onyx dish found in Hadrian's Villa at Tivoli, or, according to others, in his tomb at Rome. It has a cameo on both sides. Outside, the head of Medusa; inside, figures in relief, representing the festival held on the foundation of the city of Alexandria. 27647. A magnifying-glass. An hour can be well spent in examining this unique collection.

We now retrace our way through the Picture Gallery. On the landing of the stairs is the entrance to

THE LIBRARY,

open from 8 till 2, containing 200,000 volumes and 4,000 manuscripts. The great hall has a curious repeating echo.

Crossing the landing, and ascending the stairs on the right, is the

COLLECTION OF PAPYRI.

About three thousand were found in the ruins; almost six hundred have been unrolled and printed.

Opposite is a room containing

FOOD FROM POMPEII,

with copies of frescoes on the walls. 84595. Bread found in an oven. 84613. Grain. 84628. Dried fruits. 84839. Meat and fruit.

BREAD FOUND AT POMPEII.

84846. Glass jar with petrified wine. 84849. Glass vases with oil. *In centre:*—Glass jar containing olive oil. Strip of asbestos cloth.

Beyond is the

SECOND PICTURE GALLERY,

arranged in halls of various schools, having each separate catalogues,—Roman, Parmesan, Lombardian, Venetian, Mixed Schools, Hall of Correggio, Room of Raphael. The light in the halls devoted to the pictures in the museum is very bad, and consequently the subjects cannot be well seen.

ROMAN SCHOOL.—9. Holy Family, by Sassoferrato. 10. Temple of Vespasian and Arch of Augustus at Rome, by Pannini. 20. Madonna del Passeggio; 26. Virgin, Jesus, and S. John; 28. Madonna and Child; 30. Urban IV.—all by the school of Raphael. 21. The Saviour's Cradle and Angels, by Pinturicchio. 27. Same, by Sassoferrato. 41. "Touch me not," by F. Vanni. 54. Same, by D'Arpino.

PARMESAN SCHOOL.—1. Angel with Lance, by Simon Vovet. 3. Angel releasing Peter, by Storer. 12. Madonna and Jesus, by

Parmigiano. 18. Christ Crowned, by Correggio. 20. The Laughing Boys, by Parmigiano. 21. Cupid Resting, by Schidone. 28. S. Lawrence, by same. 40. The Sleeping Baptist, by Castiglione.

LOMBARD SCHOOL.—1. Pope Paul the Third's Shoemaker, by Schidone. 10. Christ telling the Pharisees to pay Tribute, by Schidone. 12. Amerigo Vespucci, by Parmigiano. 15. Devotees, by Leonardo da Vinci. 17. Adoration of the Magi, by Cæsare da Sesto. 18. Jesus and John, by Boltraflio. 26. Minerva, style of Parmigiano.

VENETIAN SCHOOL.—Virgin with Child and Nuns, by Luigi Vivarini. 2. Jupiter on a Globe with Divinities. 4. Jupiter at a Banquet of Deities, school of Tintoretto. Madonna and Jesus with Saints, by Bartolommeo Vivarini, 1465 A.D. 10. Church at Venice, by Canaletti (Bernardo Bellotti). 20. Paul III., by Titian, a sketch. 23. The Circumcision, by P. Veronese. 30. An Old Man, by Torbido (il Moro). 40. The Resurrection, school of Andrea Mantegna. 43. Martyrdom of S. Lawrence, a beautiful work attributed to Santacroce. 53. Christ before Herod (Luke xxiii. 7), by Andrea Schiavone. 60. Holy Family, school of Titian.

SALA DI CORREGGIO.—1. Jesus and the Doctors, by Salvator Rosa. 3. Madonna del Coniglio, the Zingarella, by Correggio. 5. Jupiter, in the form of a Shower of Gold, visiting Danaë, by Titian. 7. Marriage of S. Catherine, a gem, by Correggio. 8. Paul III., by Titian. 15. The Magdalen, by Guercino.

VARIOUS SCHOOLS.—2. S. Sebastian, by Schidone. 3. Raising of Lazarus, by Giacomo da Ponte (il Bassano). 5. Madonna del Gatto, by Giulio Romano. 7. Transfiguration, by Bellini. 8. Christopher Columbus, school of Raphael. 10. Copy of Michael Angelo's Last Judgment, by M. Venusti. 11. Virgin and Child, by Perugino. 14. Crucifixion, by Bernardino Gatti. 17. The Cavalier Tibaldeo, portrait, by Raphael. 19. Leo X., with Cardinals, by Raphael. 22. Holy Family, by Raphael. 28. S. Jerome Praying, by Palma il Vecchio. 30. Guardian Angel, by Domenichino. 32. Landscape, by Claude Gelée. 34. The Assumption, by Pinturicchio. 36. The Weeping Magdalen, by Titian. 47. The Race between Atalanta and Hippomenes, by Guido Reni. 57. La Disputa, by Palma, jun. 61. The Assumption, by Fra Bartolommeo.

Leaving the Museum, we take lunch at the Caffè Santangelo, in the Galleria Principe di Napoli, opposite; then resuming our ramble, follow the continuation of the Via Roma, Strada Nuova di Capodimonte, to the

VILLA AND PALAZZO DI CAPODIMONTE.

The grounds are laid out in the English style, and from them many splendid views may be had. The palace was begun in 1738, and finished in 1834. It contains some modern pictures, a catalogue of which will be found in each room; some medieval armour; and an interesting collection of Capodimonte porcelain, the manufacture of which has been discontinued for some time. In the valley below Capodimonte are the remains of a Roman aqueduct, Ponti Rossi.

On emerging from the gates, the Strada S. Gennaro, on the right, leads to the

CHURCH OF S. GENNARO (32),

founded in the eighth century, on the site where S. Januarius was buried. The inner court is decorated with frescoes, by Sabbatini, representing the life of the saint. Attached is a poorhouse.

Apply to the porter. Admission 1 lira each to

THE CATACOMBS,

which differ from those at Rome in the passages being much wider and loftier.* There are three stories; but like all the catacombs, they have been stripped of their inscriptions. A few frescoes still remain, figures of Peter and Paul, some early bishops, and ceiling paintings. These cemeteries were used for burial during the plague of 1656.

Retracing our way down the Via Roma, after passing the Piazza Dante, we turn to the left down the Strada S. Anna de' Lombardi, then to the left up the Strada S. Trinità to the

GESÙ NUOVO (12),

on the left. The front is in the Rustic style, but it is unfinished. The monument in the square was erected in 1747, and is surmounted by a statue of the Virgin in bronze.

The interior of the church has a fine effect. Over the door is a good fresco, by Solimena, representing Heliodorus being driven out of the temple. The Chapel of S. Ignatius contains statues of David and Jeremiah, by Fonsaga. In another chapel are paintings by Giordano and Guercino.

Nearly opposite, through a gateway to the right, is the

---

* See "The Roman Catacombs: Their True History; and Records of Early Christian Art." By S. Russell Forbes, Ph.D.

CHURCH OF S. CHIARA (8).

founded in 1380 by Robert the Wise of Anjou. It has been "restored" at various times, so that its original Gothic character is quite destroyed, and its frescoes, by Giotto, are nearly all whitewashed; yet it is an imposing building, rich in marbles. It contains several good monuments, particularly the one behind the high altar to King Robert, 42 feet in height.

To the right of the door in entering is a fresco of Mary and the dead Christ, by Giotto, very much damaged. *To the left*, the Trinity, by the same master; and the Madonna and Child is at an altar *up the nave to the left*. These last two are somewhat difficult to distinguish, owing to the votive offerings which nearly hide them.

No. 20 LARGO S. TRINITA MAGGIORE, the old refectory, contains a good fresco—the Miracle of the Loaves—after Giotto, supposed to be by one of his pupils. *Further down the street, on the left, is the*

CHURCH OF S. DOMENICO MAGGIORE (9).

A very handsome Gothic church of 1285, tastefully decorated: 249 feet long, 180 feet wide, and 84 feet high. It contains many monuments of Neapolitan princes, in the Renaissance style. It is the burial-place of S. Thomas Aquinas, who was a brother of the adjoining monastery; and they show his cell, chair, etc., also the crucifix which spoke to him: "Bene scripsisti de me, Thoma: quam ergo mercedem recipies?" to which he replied: "Non aliam nisi te."

In front of the church is an obelisk to S. Dominic.

Leaving the church by a small door opposite that by which we entered, descending the steps, we take the Vico S. Severo opposite, then the first turning on the left, Calata di S. Severo. No. 15 is the

CAPPELLA DI S. SEVERO

(*key at caffe opposite, fee half-lira*), erected in 1590 as a burial-place of the Sangro family, and noted for its allegories sculptured in marble. The man in the net, *to right of altar*, disentangling himself by the aid of Reason, represented as a crowned genius, is called *Il disinganno*. It is by Queiroli, alluding to Antonio di Sangro, who became a monk on the death of his wife Cecilia Gaetani, *to left of altar*, who is represented as Prudence slightly veiled and draped, by Conradini. At the base of her pedestal, *to left of altar*, is a dead Christ laid out in a winding-sheet, through which the anatomy of the body is distinctly shown.

Regaining the Piazza Trinità, take, to the left, the Calata Trinità Maggiore; passing the fountain on the left, steps lead up to the

CHURCH OF S. ANNA DE' LOMBARDI,
OR MONTE OLIVETO (25),

erected in 1414 by Guerello Origlia. It contains some interesting family monuments, and a chapel of the Holy Sepulchre. The group is in terra-cotta, by Modanino. Round the dead Christ are six kneeling figures, portraits of friends of the sculptor : Alphonso II. as Joseph, Pontanus as Nicodemus, Sannazzaro as Joseph of Arimathæa.

In the adjacent monastery—now public offices—Tasso was received in 1588, when in poverty.

Returning as far as the Fountain, which is surmounted with a statue of Charles III., designed by Cafaro in 1668, we turn to the right, past the Post Office, down the Strada Monteoliveto. We now reach the Strada Medina, opposite the Statue of Mercadante. On the right, next to No. 49, a flight of steps leads down to the

CHURCH OF L'INCORONATA (18),

founded by Johanna I. in 1352, and containing some good frescoes of the school of Giotto, representing the Seven Sacraments and the Church. *Over the right window*, Triumph of the Church, in which King Robert and his son Charles are introduced. Baptism : the two half figures represent Laura and Petrarch. Matrimony, containing a portrait of Dante.

Another chapel contains frescoes of the coronation and marriage of Johanna. *Opposite is the*

PALAZZO FONDI.

(*Special permission of the Prince.*) The principal pictures are four landscapes by Salvator Rosa ; the Poet Marini, by Domenichino ; S. Philip Neri, by Leonardo da Vinci ; Mater Dolorosa, by Raphael ; Portrait of Vandyck, by himself ; Madonna del Cardellino, by Rubens ; Diana and Callisto, by Rembrandt.

NEAPOLITAN LIFE.

In our rambles in Naples and its neighbourhood we can take advantage of the life and movement in the streets to study many of the phases of Neapolitan life. Such characteristics as are not exhibited in any other European city present themselves to the eye—a blending of the Oriental and the Greek. The handsome and graceful forms of the men and women, as they flit hither and thither—talking, shouting, and gesticulating—attract the attention, and show that all are not lazy, whatever some may be. Their conversation is marked with ardour; but ignorance and superstition are the chief characteristics of the mind—one moment invoking the aid of the Madonna or a saint, and the next cursing the object of their prayer. In barter keen, of amusement devotees, no opportunity is lost for business or pleasure by these sons of the sunny South.

NAPLES A ROMAN COLONY.

In July 1890 some inscriptions were found on the Corso Garibaldi showing that Elagabalus had made Naples a Roman colony.

COLONIA . AVRELIA . AVG
ANTONIANA . FELIX
NEAPOLIS.

Imp . caes . m . avrellio . Antonino
invicto . pio . felici . avg . pont
max . trib . pot . cos . p . p . divi . septimi
severi . pii . nepoti . divi . antonini
magni   pii   filio

RAMBLE II.

PIAZZA DEI MARTIRI—THEATRE OF S. CARLO—PIAZZA DEL MUNICIPIO—CHURCH OF S. GIACOMO DEGLI SPAGNUOLI—FONTANA MEDINA—CASTEL NUOVO—TRIUMPHAL ARCH—CHURCH OF S. BARBARA—PORTA DEL CARMINE—S. MARIA DEL CARMINE—PIAZZA DEL MERCATO—CORSO GARIBALDI—PORTA CAPUANA—THE CEMETERIES—CASTLE CAPUANO—SS. APOSTOLI—S. PAOLO MAGGIORE, TEMPLE OF CASTOR AND POLLUX—THEATRE—S. LORENZO, BASILICA AUGUSTALIS—THE CATHEDRAL OF S. JANUARIUS, TEMPLE OF NEPTUNE — S. RESTITUTA, TEMPLE OF APOLLO — ANCIENT THEATRE (?)—S. MARTINO—CASTEL S. ELMO—CORSO VITTORIO EMANUELE—THE INTERNATIONAL HOSPITAL—VIRGIL'S TOMB—RIVIERA DI CHIAJA—VILLA NAZIONALE—THE AQUARIUM—IMPROVEMENTS.

To the left, or west of the Pizzofalcone, the Chiatamone takes us into the Strada della Pace, hence to the

PIAZZA DEI MARTIRI.
(*Square of the Martyrs.*)

The lofty column was erected to the martyrs of Italian liberty. It is decorated with trophies, and surmounted with a figure of Victory. The four lions at its base represent the four principal revolutions in Naples. The granite pillar was originally given by the Emperor of Russia to Ferdinand of Naples.

The Strada S. Caterina to the right, and the Strada di Chiaja to the right, lead to the Piazza S. Ferdinando and the

THEATRE OF S. CARLO (35).
(*Teatro S. Carlo.*)

Built in 1737 by King Charles III., and rebuilt since the fire of 1816. The façade is decorated with bas-reliefs. At the entrance are two horse-tamers, given by the Emperor Nicholas, the work of Baron Clodt.

Under the arcades you can have a love or business letter written with equal despatch.

THE GALLERIA UMBERTO.

This is a fine handsome arcade, in the form of a Greek cross, with a dome in the centre. The arms have entries from the Via S. Carlo, Via Roma, Via del Municipio, and Via S. Brigida. It contains some elegant shops and a concert-hall in the basement.

PIAZZA DEL MUNICIPIO.

Following the Via S. Carlo, we come to the fine new square which has recently been opened out from the town-hall right down to the Molo or quay. It is a grand improvement, and worthy of the largest city in Italy.

By the *Municipio* is the

CHURCH OF S. GIACOMO DEGLI SPAGNUOLI (13),

erected in 1540 by Don Pedro de Toledo, containing his Tomb, Giovanni da Nola's masterpiece. *To the right in entering* there is a good Holy Family by Andrea del Sarto; and *in the third chapel on the left* Lama's Descent from the Cross.

From the *Strada del Molo*, the *Strada Medina* leads out on the left. *In the open space is the*

FONTANA MEDINA,

(*Medina Fountain*,)

formed by a large basin supported by four satyrs. In the centre rises Neptune with his trident, from which flow refreshing streams amidst jets of water. Four tritons on sea-horses occupy the base, with lions and other animals spouting forth sprays of water.

To the right is the

CASTEL NUOVO.

(*New Castle.*)

After passing the guard at the modern entrance, turn to the right, then to the left, then to the left again. Custodian at No. 223.

Founded in 1283, and once the residence of the kings of the Houses of Anjou and Aragon; also of the Spanish viceroys.

The entrance to the castle square is formed by a lofty

TRIUMPHAL ARCH,

between two round towers, one of which has recently fallen. Corinthian columns on either side of the arch support a frieze and cornice; on the attic is the relief representing the entry of Alfonso into Naples, 1443; above are statues, with the four Virtues below in niches. The reliefs on the inside are good. The bronze doors are sculptured by a Neapolitan monk, representing the victories of Ferdinand I. In them is lodged a cannon-ball. The date of the arch is 1470. *In the castle square is the*

CHURCH OF S. BARBARA.

Custodian at No. 223, outside the arch, on the right in entering.

It has a handsome Corinthian front, with a beautiful relief of the Madonna over the entrance, by Majano. Behind the high altar is the famous oil-painting of the Adoration of the Magi, considered by Vasari to be by Van Eyck, and one of the oldest paintings in the world. In an adjoining chapel are some good paintings on the vault and altar.

We resume our ramble along the Strada del Molo and Strada del Piliero, which skirt the harbours. Visitors can ascend to the top of the lighthouse on the Molo, where a good view of the town can be had. Fee, 1 lira.

The Strada Nuova Quay leads to the PORTA DEL CARMINE and CASTEL DEL CARMINE, now a prison and barracks, once occupied by Masaniello. *In the adjoining piazza is the*

CHURCH OF S. MARIA DEL CARMINE (20),

containing a beautiful statue by Thorwaldsen, erected in 1847 by Maximilian II. of Bavaria to his ancestor, King Couradin, the last of the Hohenstauffen, who was executed in the adjacent PIAZZA DEL MERCATO in 1268 by order of Charles I. of Anjou.

To the right we pass up the Corso Garibaldi to the Porta Capuana, outside which are the Cemeteries.

THE PORTA CAPUANA,

re-erected in 1535, is one of the finest Renaissance gateways in existence, and is flanked by two picturesque round towers. *Through it is* the CASTEL CAPUANA, formerly the residence of the kings, but now the Courts of Justice. *From the Strada dei Tribunali, on the right, we turn up the Strada Santi Apostoli to the*

CHURCH OF SS. APOSTOLI (6),

founded by Constantine on the ruins of a temple of Mercury, and rebuilt in 1626. This church has a pleasing effect, with its decorations of various coloured marbles and frescoes by some of the best Neapolitan masters : the cupola by Lanfranco and Benasca, the nave by Solimena, and the transept by Giordano. The Pool of Bethesda, *over the door*, is by Lanfranco.

Regaining the *Strada dei Tribunali*, *a little beyond*, *on the right*, *is the*

CHURCH OF S. PAOLO MAGGIORE (26),

on the site of the ancient Temple of Castor and Pollux ; erected by Julius Tarsus, Prefect of Naples under Augustus. Two beautiful Corinthian columns, supporting a piece of the architrave, still remain ; also the bases of two others.

The church is approached by a lofty flight of steps, and was destroyed by an earthquake in 1688, but has been rebuilt. *To the left* of the front is a statue to S. Gaetano Tiene.

THE ROMAN THEATRE.

The CLOISTERS, *entered from the Strada S. Paolo on the left of the church*, *through an archway on the right*, are formed by twenty-four ancient granite columns, which are supposed to have formed part of a theatre in which Nero acted. At the back of the church is another cloister, the vaults of which are said to be part of the theatre, which is thus spoken of by Suetonius (" Nero," xx.) :—

"Accordingly, he made his first public appearance at Naples ; and although the theatre quivered with the sudden shock of an earthquake, he did not desist until he had finished the piece of music he had begun. He played and sang in the same place several times, and for several days together, taking only now and then a little respite to refresh his voice. Impatient of retirement, it was his custom to go from the bath to the theatre ; and after dining in the orchestra amidst a crowded assembly of the people, he promised them in Greek 'that after he had drunk a little he would give them a tune which would make their ears tingle.' Being highly pleased with the songs that were sung in his praise by some Alexandrians belonging to the fleet just arrived at Naples, he sent for more of the like singers from Alexandria. At the same time he chose young men of the equestrian order, and above five thousand robust young fellows from the common people, on purpose to learn various kinds of applause, called *bombi*, *imbrices*, and *testæ*, which they were to practise in his favour whenever he performed. They were divided into several parties, and were remarkable for their fine heads of hair, and were extremely well dressed, with rings upon their left hands.

The leaders of these bands had salaries of forty thousand sesterces allowed them."

"The theatre, when the audience had retired, being empty, fell into a heap of ruins without hurting any one" (Tacitus, "Ann." xv. 34).

Upon a pier of the arch of one of the vomitoria this inscription has been recently discovered—ΜΝΗϹΟΗΠΕΚΟΥΛΙΑΡΙϹ.

Nearly opposite S. Paolo, to the left, is the

CHURCH OF S. LORENZO MAGGIORE (10),

(*S. Lawrence,*)

with a massive square belfry adjoining, on the site of the ancient Basilica Augustalis, which, up to 1266, was the meeting-place of the Neapolitan senate. It was suppressed by Charles of Anjou and turned into a church; but the portal, choir, and two beautiful windows in the cloisters are the only Gothic parts left. It contains monuments of the Neapolitan kings. In the adjoining monastery Petrarch resided in 1343; and it was in this church that Boccacio beheld his beautiful Fiammetta, a princess of the period. The arch of the transept and the vault of the tribunal, behind the altar, are the only parts visible of the ancient Roman basilica.

Retracing our steps a short way, we enter the new Strada del Duomo. Turning down it to the left, on the opposite side, is the

CATHEDRAL OF S. JANUARIUS (1),

supposed to be erected on the site of a temple to Neptune. The font, an ancient vase of Egyptian Casalta marble with a porphyry pedestal, was anciently dedicated to Bacchus. The cathedral is approached by a flight of steps. It is of the Gothic order, and was founded in 1272. Nearly destroyed by the earthquake of 1456, it has been since restored. It is built in the basilica form, and presents a magnificent appearance. There are many tombs and monuments of interest. Below the high altar is the confessional of S. Januarius (*entrance to right, down steps; fee, half-lira*), formed with ancient columns and marbles, to the left side of which is the kneeling figure of Cardinal Carafa. There are several pieces of ancient sculpture worked into the panels.

On entering the cathedral, the third chapel in the right aisle is that known as the Cappella del Tesoro, having a marble façade and grand bronze doors, with columns of verde antico (green marble). The interior is in the form of a Greek cross, and is embellished with pictures on copper by Domenichino, Guido Reni, and Lanfranco.

There are a silver bust of the saint, forty-five silver busts of other saints, and several valuable relics. Forty-two columns of brocatello support the different altars. Here is deposited the blood of the saint, martyred under Diocletian, and which liquefies on the first Sunday in May, 19th September, and 16th December, which are great festivals with the Neapolitans.

Opposite, entered from the cathedral, door in left aisle—fee, half-lira, —is the

CHURCH OF S. RESTITUTA,

on the site of, and erected out of the remains of, a temple to Apollo, the Corinthian columns of which form the nave of the church, which is of the basilica form. It contains an ancient mosaic of the Virgin, two reliefs from a chancel screen, each in fifteen compartments. Adjoining is the Chapel of S. Giovanni *in fonte*. It was formerly the baptistery. Said to be founded by Constantine in 333. The vault is formed of ancient mosaics, the centre being the monogram of Christ, formed by the two first letters X (ki) P (row) of the Greek word.

In the Strada Anticaglia, to the right of the cathedral, then to the left, are some remains called a theatre.

THE ANCIENT BATHS.

The remains consist of two massive walls of brick-work at right angles to one another, and they are pierced by two arches, under which passes the modern street. The construction proves them to belong to the latter part of the second century. What they formed part of seems to us uncertain; but they certainly do not form the component parts of a theatre. Perhaps they were baths.

Lunch should be taken in this locality.

We here enter our carriage, and passing by the gardens of the Piazza Cavour, the Strada Salvator Rosa takes us up to the

CHURCH AND MONASTERY OF S. MARTINO.

Open from 9 till 5; entrance, 1 lira each. To save time, the carriage can be told to return and wait at the foot of the descent, which can be best made on foot.

Formerly belonging to the Carthusians, but now to the government. Com. Fiorelli has recently collected within its walls a museum of majolicas, tapestry, glasses, mirrors, etc. For its decorations and richness the church is unsurpassed. Twelve different roses of Egyptian granite, a mosaic pavement, a high altar, and paintings render it superb.

The vault has a painting of the Ascension, with the twelve apostles between the entrance (the Descent from the Cross is by Stanzioni); an unfinished Nativity by Guido Reni, who died whilst at work on the subject. In the *tesoro* of the sacristy is Spagnoletto's masterpiece, the Descent from the Cross. The Judith on its vault, by Giordano, is said to have been painted in forty-eight hours when he was seventy-two years old.

Grand views from the belvedere.

THE CASTEL S. ELMO.

(*Permission, see page 8.*) Formerly a simple tower, then a fortress, and now a barrack and prison. Contains numerous underground passages and vaults, where men were confined under the Bourbons.

From the ramparts a most glorious panoramic view may be enjoyed.

Descending by the steps, or returning by the same road by which we came, to the Piazza Salvator Rosa, we turn to the right, down the new

CORSO VITTORIO EMANUELE,

the finest and most commanding drive of any town in Europe, skirting round the hills of S. Elmo and Posilipo—the far-famed bay, Vesuvius, and the city being interviewed and enjoyed with ease. It is two miles and a half long.

THE INTERNATIONAL HOSPITAL.

"Visitors to Naples will be delighted to know that there is now a comfortable hospital for them to fall back upon in the unfortunate event of their becoming ill. The new building for the old International Hospital, Villa Bentinck—at first only for a limited number of patients until the new additional wings are perfectly dry—is in a most salubrious and charming situation, at the junction of the Corso Vittorio Emanuele and the new Via Tasso, on the slope of the Vomero. All the windows command splendid views of the Bay of Naples or the surrounding hills. It has a large garden, full of flowers, orange and lemon trees, and on all sides are blossoming orchards and vineyards. The building to which the hospital is now removed was not obtained, nor the additional wings and improvements carried out, without great financial sacrifices. The capital bequeathed by the late Lady Bentinck for the purpose of building a new house was not entirely absorbed, but the committee had to take upon themselves the payment of the interest on a considerable sum needed for the adaptation of the former Villa Rossi, now renamed Villa Bentinck, to the uses of a hospital. The enlargements and improvements have been admirably executed by a resident English engineer, Mr. Lamont Young. The report of the committee for the year 1883 shows that the usefulness of the hospital is constantly increasing. In consequence of the change of house, etc., a deficit of 31,700 francs has now to be provided for, and the committee trust— considering the increase of patients and gratuitous consultations (given to three hundred and sixteen persons, of whom forty-two were English mariners), which have more than trebled since 1878, when the hospital was founded—that many societies and private persons who have profited by the institution may become liberal subscribers in future, and help the hospital through the serious financial difficulties it has now to overcome. The comfort, good nursing, and first-rate medical advice afforded by the institution to all travellers who may be ill while staying in Naples are beyond price. In an hotel a patient not only suffers from careless and insufficient nursing and ill-prepared food, but he is put to extravagant expense and subject to many annoyances, all of which are avoided if he takes refuge in case of sickness in the International Hospital. Many well-to-do travellers have passed safely and peacefully through severe illness under the affectionate care of the resident physician, Dr. Malbrane, and have been so well satisfied with the care and comfort that surrounded them that they were almost sorry to leave the house; and the latter fact is universally true of English sailors, who find a real home in the hospital under the kind superintendence of the directress, Miss Fellmann. The institution is worthy of all support from rich travellers, who, when ill in an hotel, are subject to the exorbitance of the proprietors and to a thousand other discomforts."

"It may be well to mention the terms of the different classes, which include pension, medical advice, and nursing, etc. :— First class, 15 francs ; second class, 6 francs ; and third class, 2 francs 50 centesimi per day. Sailors pay a reduced price of 1 franc 80 centesimi a day for the third class, and it is contemplated to receive them gratis in future. Admission is obtained through the British or American consul. Subscriptions from visitors for this good work are earnestly requested."

At the end of the Corso Vittorio Emanuele we turn to the right, passing the CHURCH OF S. MARIA DI PIEDIGROTTA. *Between the smithy, Nos. 8 and 9, is a door leading to a flight of steps. In the vineyard above is*

VIRGIL'S TOMB.

Admission, 1 lira. The poet died at Brundisium 19 B.C., and expressed his desire to be buried on his estate at Posilipo, where he had written the "Georgics" and part of the "Æneid." Tradition says this is his tomb, and once contained this epitaph, by Virgil himself, which was (1840) replaced by a modern copy:—

> IN MANTUA BORN, BUT IN CALABRIA BRED,
> FAIR NAPLES OWNS ME NOW: THE PASTORAL CHARGE,
> AND AGRICULTURAL TOILS, AND ARMS I SUNG.

It is also stated that a stone was found here some time since, on which was the inscription—

> STOP, TRAVELLER, AND READ A FEW WORDS—
> HERE LIES MARO.

The tomb is a chamber sixteen feet square, with a vaulted roof, and lighted by three windows. In the reticulated walls are ten columbaria for cinerary urns. Virgil's is said to have stood in the centre, supported by nine marble pillars. This was in 1326; but it has now entirely disappeared. In 1553 the following inscription was put up:—

> QUI CINERES ? TUMULI HÆC VESTIGIA : CONDITUR OLIM
> ILLE HIC QUI CECINIT PASCUA, RURA, DUCES.

The view from the top of the tomb is uninteresting; but from above the tomb, in the garden, a fine view may be had (see *frontispiece*), which is thus described by the poet Statius ("Syl." iv. 4):—

> "Lo! idly wandering on the sea-beat strand,
> Where the famed Siren on Ausonia's land
> First moored her bark, I strike the sounding string;
> At Virgil's honoured tomb I sit and sing.
> Warmed by the hallowed spot, my muse takes fire,
> And sweeps with bolder hand my humble lyre.
> These strains, Marcellus, on the Chalcian shores
> I penned, when great Vesuvius smokes and roars,
> And from his crater ruddy flames expires,
> With fury scarce surpassed by Etna's fires."

Silius Italicus became possessed of this property and of the adjoining Villa of Cicero. Pliny, jun. (iii. 6), tells us Silius starved himself to death here, and that "he celebrated the anniversary of Virgil's birth-day with more solemnity than his own, especially at

FOUNTAIN IN THE VILLA NAZIONALE.

Naples, where he used to approach his tomb with as much veneration as if it had been a temple." Martial (xi. 51) says—

> "To honour Maro's dust and sacred shade
> One swain remained, deserted, poor, alone,
> Till Silius came his pious toils to aid
> In homage to a name scarce greater than his own."

Descend from the tomb to the

RIVIERA DI CHIAJA AND VILLA NAZIONALE.

La Chiaja, as it is called, is the finest street and the Rotten Row of Naples. One side is occupied by houses, and the other by the National Park (Villa Nazionale), the favourite resort of visitors and natives. In the central path there is an antique basin from Pæstum. All the sculptures are modern, as also the memorials to Virgil and Tasso. The municipal band plays in the winter from 3 P.M. till 5, and in the summer till 9 P.M. In the grounds is The AQUARIUM, open from 9 till 5. *Admission—summer, 1 lira; winter, 2 lire.*

RAMBLE III.

TORRE DEL GRECO—TORRE DELL' ANNUNZIATA—POMPEII—HISTORICAL NOTICES—THE DESTRUCTION OF POMPEII—SYNOPSIS OF RAMBLE—IMPRESSIONS—CAMALDOLI.

TORRE DEL GRECO,

on the coast, about 8 miles from Naples, has been repeatedly destroyed by Vesuvius. Under the lava of the eruptions of 79 and 1631, at Torre del Greco, have been discovered the remains of an aqueduct, a water reservoir, and a caldarium. The buildings seem to have formed part of *thermæ*. Torre del Greco is noted for its coral manufactory, good air, and "Lachrymæ Christi" wine, grown on the slopes of the volcano, and called from its quality the Tears of Christ.

Beyond is

TORRE DELL' ANNUNZIATA,

12 miles from Naples, and the junction of the Pompeii and Castellamare line.

There is nothing of interest in the town itself.

POMPEII.

By rail is the best way of getting to Pompeii; it is likewise the least expensive. As the trains are liable to alterations, it is best to consult local time-tables. Fares, 5, 4, and 2 lire return. Take lunch. Arriving at the station, a path leads straight up to the entrance. On the left is the Hotel Diomède, a fair place for lunch, after seeing the ruins, if

*you have not brought it with you. Admission, including guide, 2 lire.
Sundays free.*

It is well known to students that the exact date of the destruction of Pompeii and Herculaneum has been disputed : some manuscripts of Pliny's celebrated letters read "Nonum Kalend Septemb.," which would be August 23rd, 79 ; but one manuscript reads "Non November," which would be November 5th, 79. The earlier date was the more generally accepted one of the two, but the later date is now proved to be the correct one.

Dion Cassius says the eruption took place in the autumn, without giving the exact date ; this is confirmed from the fact that fruits and nuts were found in the ruins which could not have been there if the city was destroyed in August.

On the 11th of October 1889, outside the Porta Stabiana, the bodies of two men and a woman were found, and by them a tree. These objects were treated in the usual way to obtain the casts, the tree showing remains of leaves and fruit. The botanist, Professor Fortunato Pasquale, examined the remains, and pronounces the tree to be a variety of the *Laurus nobilis;* that is the *arbutus* or *unedo* or strawberry-tree, the fruit of which does not ripen till well into November. The fruit found was immature, and proves that the tree must have fallen early in November.

The fruit consists of a small round red ball, the coat of which is somewhat rough. It grows in profusion at the Lakes of Killarney, and ripens about Christmas. The fruit is sold in the streets of Rome in December, under the title of *ceresa marine;* in Florence the fruit is called *corbezzola;* and at Siena, *albatre.* Pliny says (xxiii. 79) : "The arbutus or unedo bears a fruit that is difficult of digestion and injurious to the stomach." "The fruit is held in no esteem, in proof of which it has gained its name of unedo (*unum edo,* I eat but one), people being generally content with eating but one" (xv. 28).

From this interesting discovery we are now certain that Pompeii was destroyed on November 5th, 79.

BIBLIOGRAFIA DI POMPEI.

The literature about Pompeii has been collated by Mr. F. Furchheim of Naples, and described in his "Bibliografia di Pompei Ercolano e Stabia," 2nd edition, 1891. It contains over five hundred works in Latin, Italian, English, French, and German.

MAP OF POMPEII.

HISTORICAL NOTICES.

Strabo (v. iv. 8) says, "Pompeii, on the river Sarnus, was originally held by the Osci, then by the Tyrrhenians and Pelasgians, then by the Samnites, who in their turn were expelled by the Romans. It is the port of Nola, Nuceria, and Acerræ, being situated on the river Sarnus, which is suited for the exportation and importation of cargoes."

Tacitus ("Ann." xv. 22) records an earthquake in 63 A.D., from which it seems the town had not recovered at its final destruction. "Pompeii, a celebrated town of Campania, was overthrown by an earthquake."

"Claudius lost his son Drusus at Pompeii when he was very young, he being choked with a pear, which in his play he tossed into the air and caught in his mouth" (Suetonius, "Claudius," xxvii.).

"Pompeii, from which Mount Vesuvius may be seen at no great distance, and which is watered by the river Sarnus" (Pliny, iii. 9).

During the Catiline conspiracy, Publius Sylla established a military colony just outside the gate of Herculaneum, and this was augmented by Augustus, and called PAGUS AUGUSTUS FELIX.

The settlement of this colony by Publius Sylla was one of the charges brought against him when he was defended by Cicero, who says (xxi.), "Though that colony was originally settled by Publius Sylla, and though the fortune of the Roman people has separated the interests of the settlers from the fortunes of the native citizens of Pompeii, he is still so popular among and so much beloved by both parties, that he seems not so much to have dispossessed the one party of their lands as to have settled both of them in that country."

The grand catastrophe, which took place on November 5th, 79 A.D., is fortunately described to us by Pliny, jun., in his letters (vi. 17, 20) to Tacitus the historian.

THE DESTRUCTION OF POMPEII.

PLINY TO TACITUS.

"Your request that I would send you an account of my uncle's death, in order to transmit a more exact relation of it to posterity, merits my acknowledgments; for if the glorious circumstances which occasioned this accident shall be celebrated by your pen, the manner of his exit will be rendered for ever illustrious. Notwithstanding he perished by a misfortune, which, as it involved at the same time a most beautiful country in ruins, and destroyed so many populous cities, seems to promise him an everlasting remembrance; notwithstanding he has himself composed many works which will descend to the latest times, yet I am persuaded the mentioning of him in your immortal writings will greatly contribute to eternalize his name. Happy I deem those to be whom the gods have distinguished with the abilities either of performing such actions as are worthy of being related, or of relating them in a manner worthy of being read. But doubly happy are they who are blessed with both these uncommon endowments; and in that number my uncle, as his own writings and your history will prove, may justly be ranked. It is with extreme willingness, therefore, I execute your commands; and I should, indeed, have claimed the task if you had not enjoined it.

"He was at that time, with the fleet under his command, at Misenum. On the 5th of November, about one in the afternoon, my mother desired him to observe a cloud which appeared of a very unusual size and shape. He had just returned from enjoying the benefit of the sun, and after bathing in cold water and taking a slight repast, had retired to his study. He immediately arose and went out upon an eminence, from whence he might more distinctly view this very singular phenomenon. It was not at that distance discernible from what mountain this cloud issued, but it was found afterwards to proceed from Vesuvius. I cannot give you a more exact description of its figure than by resembling it to that of a pine tree; for it shot up a great height in the form of a tall trunk, which spread at the top into sort of branches, occasioned by, I suppose, either that the force of the internal vapour which impelled the cloud upwards decreased in strength as it advanced, or that the cloud, being pressed back by its own weight, expanded itself in the manner I have mentioned. It appeared sometimes bright and sometimes dark and spotted, as it was either more or less impregnated with earth and cinders. This uncommon appearance excited my uncle's philosophical curiosity to take a nearer view of it. He accordingly ordered a light vessel to be prepared, and offered me the liberty, if I thought proper, to attend him. I rather chose to continue the employment in which I was engaged; for it happened that he had given me a certain writing to copy. As he was going out of the house with his tablets in his hand, he was met by the mariners belonging to the galleys stationed at Retina, from which they had fled in the utmost terror; for that port being situated at the foot of Vesuvius, they had no other way to escape than by sea. They conjured him, therefore, not to proceed and expose his life to imminent and inevitable danger. In compliance with their advice he changed his original intention, and instead of gratifying his philosophical spirit, he resigned it to the more magnanimous principle of aiding the distressed. With this view he ordered the fleet immediately to put to sea, and went himself on board with an intention of assisting not only Retina, but the several other towns which stood thick upon that beautiful coast. Hastening to the place, therefore, from whence others fled with the utmost terror, he steered his direct course to the point of danger, and with so much calmness and presence of mind as to be able to make and dictate his observations upon the appearance and progress of that dreadful scene. He was now so near the mountain that the cinders, which grew thicker and hotter the more he advanced, fell into the ships, together with pumice-stones and black pieces of burning rock. They were likewise in danger, not only of being aground by the sudden retreat of the sea, but also from the vast fragments which rolled down from the mountains and obstructed all the shore. Here he stopped to consider whether he should return back, to which the pilot advising him,—'Fortune,' said he, 'befriends the brave; steer to Pomponianus.' Pomponianus was then at Stabiæ, separated by a gulf, which the sea, after several insensible windings, forms upon that shore. Pomponianus had already sent his baggage on board; for though he was not at that time in actual danger, yet being within the view of it, and indeed extremely near, he was determined, if it should in the least increase, to put to sea as soon as the wind should change. It was favourable, however, for carrying my uncle to Pomponianus, whom he found in the greatest consternation; and embracing him with tenderness, he encouraged and exhorted him to keep up his spirits. The more to dissipate his fears, he ordered his servants, with an air of unconcern, to carry him to the baths; and after having bathed, he sat down to supper with great (or at least, what is equally heroic, with all the appearance of) cheerfulness.

"In the meanwhile, the fire from Vesuvius flamed forth from several parts of the mountain with great violence, which the darkness of the night contributed to render still more visible and dreadful. But my uncle, in order to calm the apprehensions of his friend, assured him it was only the conflagration of the villages, which the country people had abandoned. After this he retired to rest, and it is most certain he was so little discomposed as to fall into a deep sleep; for being corpulent and breathing hard, the attendants in the ante-chamber actually heard him snore. The court which led to his apartments being now almost filled with stones and ashes, it would have been impossible for him, if he had continued there any longer, to have made his way out; it was thought proper, therefore, to awaken him. He got up and joined Pomponianus and the rest of the company, who had not been sufficiently unconcerned to think of going to bed. They consulted together whether it would be most prudent to trust to the houses, which now shook from side to side with frequent and violent concussions, or flee to the open fields, where the calcined stones and cinders, though levigated indeed, yet fell in large showers, and threatened them with instant destruction. In this distress they resolved for the fields as the less dangerous situation of the two—a resolution which, while the rest of the company were hurried into by their fears, my uncle embraced upon cool and deliberate consideration. They went out, then, having pillows tied upon their heads with napkins, and this was their whole defence against the storm of stones that fell around them.

"It was now day everywhere else, but *there* a deeper darkness prevailed than in the blackest night, which, however, was in some degree dissipated by torches and other lights of various kinds. They thought it expedient to go down further upon the shore, in order to observe if they might safely put out to sea; but they found the waves still running extremely high and boisterous. There my uncle, having drunk a draught or two of cold water, laid himself down upon a sailcloth which was spread for him, when immediately the flames, preceded by a strong smell of sulphur, dispersed the rest of the company and obliged him to rise. He raised himself up with the assistance of two of his servants, and instantly fell down dead—suffocated, I conjecture, by some gross and noxious vapour, having always had weak lungs, and being frequently subject to a difficulty of breathing. As soon as it was light again, which was not till the third day after this melancholy accident, his body was found entire and without any marks of violence, exactly in the same posture as that in which he fell, and looking more like a man asleep than dead. During all this time my mother and I too were at Misenum.

"But this has no connection with your history, as your inquiry went no further than concerning my uncle's death; with that, therefore, I will put an end to my letter. Suffer me only to add that I have faithfully related to you what I was either an eye-witness of myself or received immediately after the accident happened, and before there was time to vary the truth. You will choose out of this narrative such circumstances as shall be most suitable to your purpose; for there is a great difference between writing a letter and composing a history, between addressing a friend and addressing the public. Farewell."

"The letter, which in compliance with your request I wrote to you concerning the death of my uncle, has raised, it seems, your curiosity to know what terrors and dangers attended me while I continued at Misenum; for there, I think, the account in my former broke off.

'Though my shocked soul recoils my tongue shall tell.'

"My uncle having left us, I continued the employment which prevented my going with him, till it was time to bathe, after which I went to supper, and then fell into a short and unquiet sleep. There had been during many days before some shocks of an earthquake, which the less alarmed us as they are frequent in Campania; but they were so particularly violent that night that they not only shook everything about us, but seemed indeed to threaten total destruction. My mother flew to my chamber, where she found me rising in order to awaken her. We went out into a small court belonging to the house, which separated the sea from the buildings. As I was at that time but eighteen years of age, I know not whether I should call my behaviour in this perilous conjuncture courage or rashness, but I took up Livy and amused myself with turning over that author, and even making extracts from him, as if I had been perfectly at my ease. While we were in this situation, a friend of my uncle's, who was just come from Spain to pay him a visit, joined us, and observing me sitting by my mother with a book in my hand, reproved her patience and my security; nevertheless, I still went on with my author.

"It was now morning, but the light was exceedingly faint and languid. The buildings all around us tottered, and though we stood upon open ground, yet as the place was narrow and confined, there was no remaining without imminent danger; we therefore resolved to leave the town. The people followed us in the utmost consternation, and (as to a mind distracted with terror every suggestion seems more prudent than its own) pressed in crowds about us in our way out. Being advanced at a convenient distance from the houses, we stood still in the midst of a most hazardous and tremendous scene. The chariots which we had ordered to be drawn out were so agitated backwards and forwards, though upon the most level ground, that we could not keep them steady, even by supporting them with large stones. The sea seemed to roll back upon itself, and to be driven from its banks by the convulsive motion of the earth; it is certain, at least, the shore was considerably enlarged, and several sea animals were left upon it. On the other side a black and dreadful cloud bursting with an igneous serpentine vapour darted out a long train of fire, resembling flashes of lightning, but much larger. Upon this our Spanish friend, whom I mentioned above, addressed himself to my mother and me with great warmth and earnestness. 'If your brother and your uncle,' said he, 'is safe, he certainly wishes you may be so too; but if he perished, it was his desire, no doubt, that you might both survive him. Why, therefore, do you delay your escape a moment?' 'We could never think of our own safety,' we replied, 'while we were uncertain of his;' upon which our friend left us and withdrew from the danger with the utmost precipitation.

"Soon afterwards the cloud seemed to descend and cover the whole ocean, as indeed it entirely hid the island of Caprea and the promontory of Misenum. My mother conjured me to make my escape at any rate, which as I was young I might easily effect; as for herself, she said, her age and corpulency rendered all attempts of that sort impossible: however, she would willingly meet death if she could have the satisfaction of seeing that she was not the occasion of mine. But I absolutely refused to leave her, and taking her by the hand I led her on. She complied with great reluctance, and not without many reproaches to herself for being the occasion of retarding my flight.

"The ashes now began to fall upon us, though in no great quantity. I turned my head, and observed behind us a thick smoke, which came rolling after us like a torrent. I proposed, while we had yet any light, to turn out of the highroad, lest she should be pressed to death in the dark by the crowd that followed us. We had scarcely stepped out of the path when darkness overspread us, not like that of a cloudy night, or when there is no moon, but like that of a room when it is shut up and all the lights extinct. Nothing then was to be heard but the shrieks of women, the screams of children, and the cries of men—some calling for their children, others for their parents, others for their husbands, and only distinguishing each other by their voices; one lamenting his own fate, another that of his family; some wishing to die from the very fear of dying; some lifting their hands to the gods; but the greater part imagining that the last and eternal night was come which was to destroy both the gods and the world together. Among these there were some who augmented the real terrors by imaginary ones, and made the frighted multitude falsely believe that Misenum was actually in flames. At length a glimmering light appeared, which we imagined to be rather the forerunner of an approaching burst of flames (as in fact it was) than the return of day; however, the fire fell at a distance from us. Then again we were immersed in thick darkness, and a heavy shower of ashes rained upon us, which we were obliged every now and then to shake off, otherwise we should have been overwhelmed and buried in the heap.

"I might boast that during all this scene of horror not a sigh or expression of fear escaped from me, had not my support been founded on that miserable though strong consolation that all mankind were involved in the same calamity, and that I imagined I was perishing with the world itself.

"At last this terrible darkness was dissipated by degrees like a cloud or smoke. The real day returned, and even the sun appeared, though very faintly, and as when an eclipse is coming on. Every object that presented itself to our eyes (which were extremely weakened) seemed changed, being covered with white ashes as with a deep snow. We returned to Misenum, where we refreshed ourselves as well as we could, and passed an anxious night between hope and fear,—though, indeed, with a much larger share of the latter; for the earth still continued to shake, while several enthusiastic persons ran wildly among the people, throwing out terrifying predictions, or making a kind of frantic sport of their own and their friends' wretched situation. However, my mother and I, notwithstanding the danger we had passed, and that which still threatened us, had no intention of leaving Misenum till we should receive some account of my uncle.

"And now you will read this narrative without any view of inserting it in your history, of which it is by no means worthy; and, indeed, you must impute it to your own request if it should appear not to deserve even the trouble of a letter. Farewell."

A RAMBLE THROUGH THE CITY OF THE DEAD.

Traces of the buried city were first discovered in 1689, but excavations were not commenced till 1721. They were carried on at irregular intervals till Naples was added to the rest of United Italy, when Signor Fiorelli was appointed director of the excavations. Since then the works have been and are being actively carried on. Every day fresh and interesting discoveries are made.

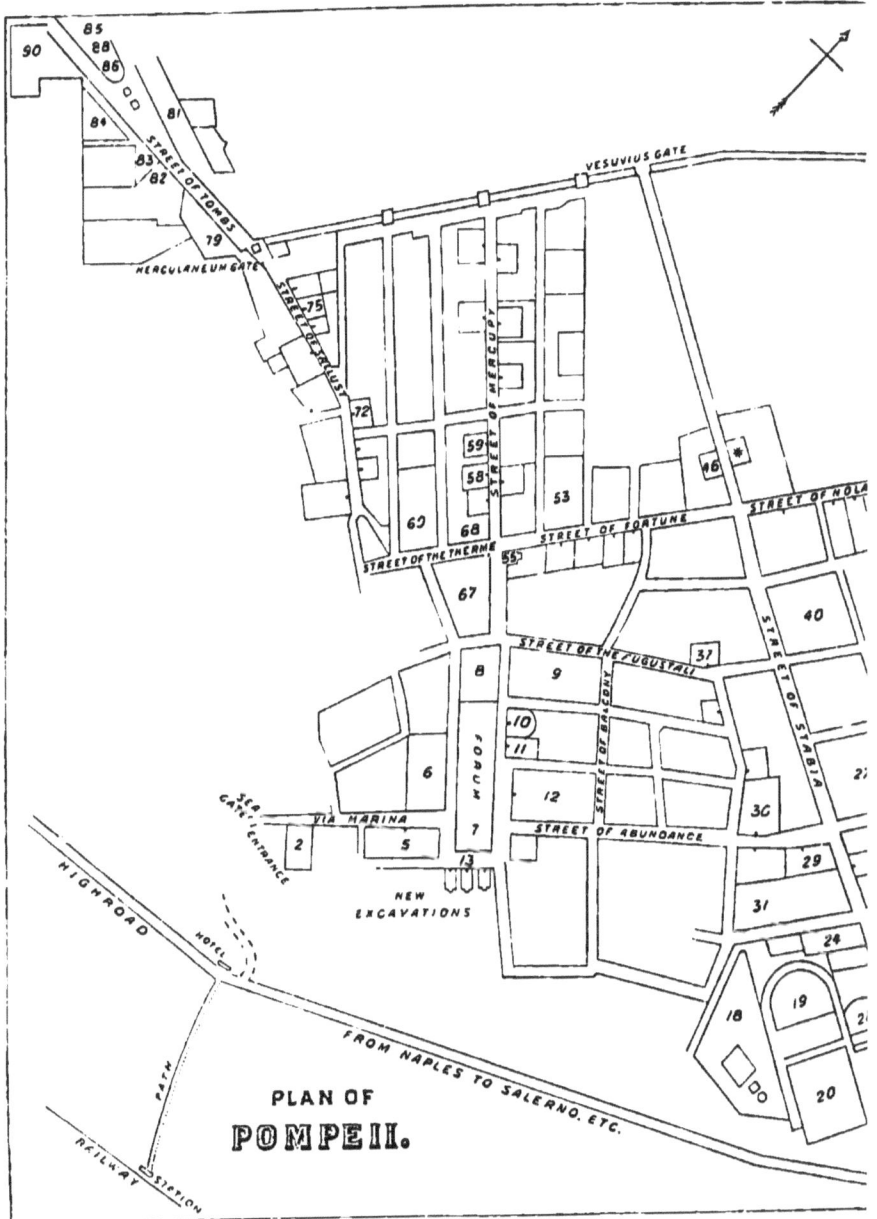

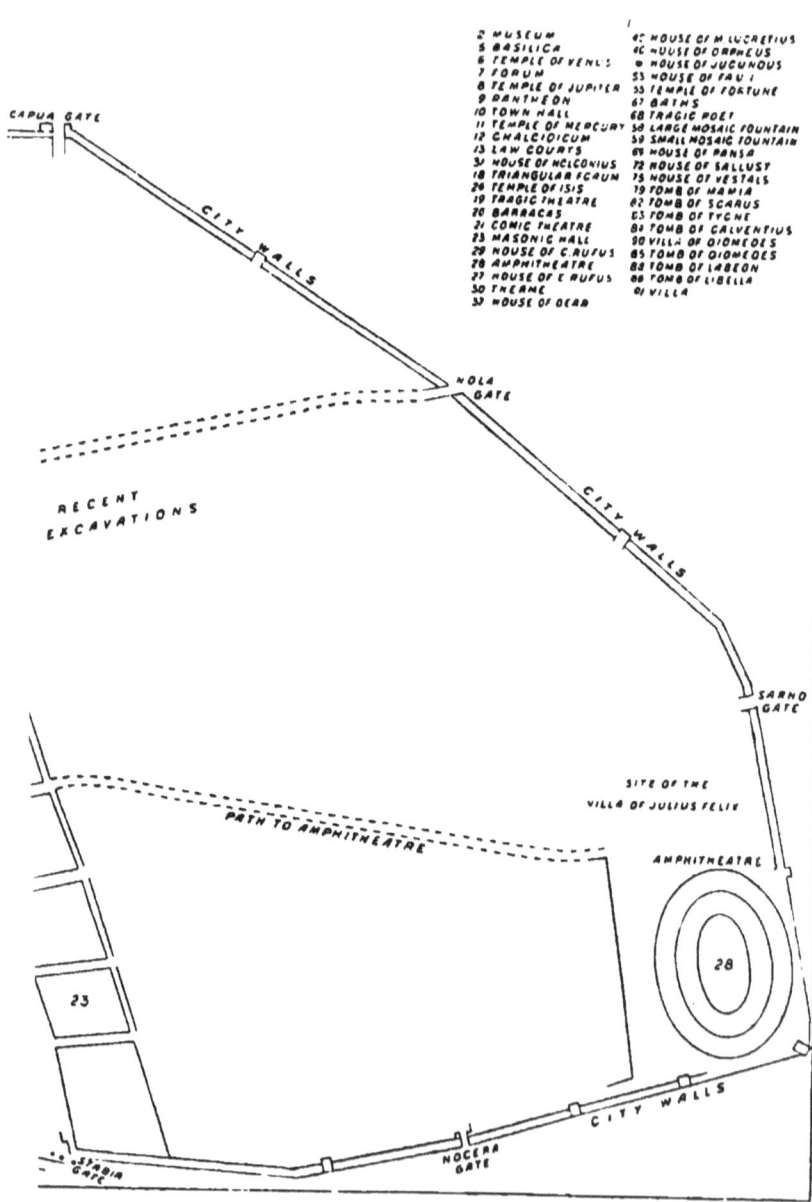

The ruined city is divided into *insulæ*, islands; and *regioni*, regions. There are nine regioni, and each block of buildings is called an insula; these are all numbered.

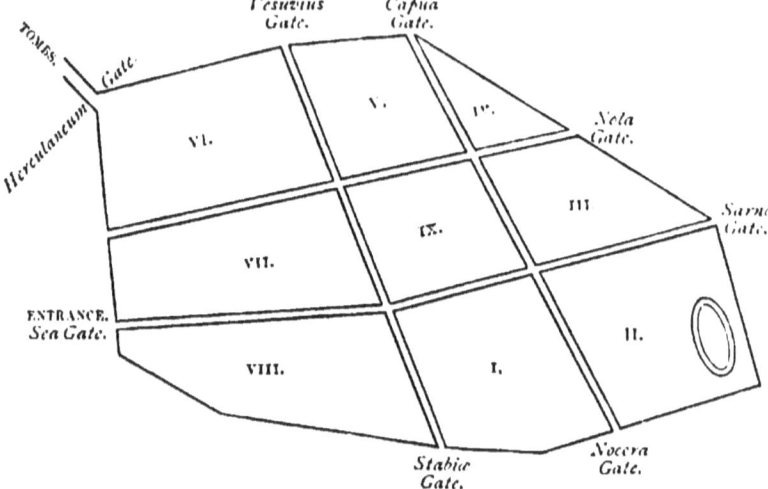

SKETCH MAP OF THE REGIONI OF POMPEII.

SYNOPSIS OF PRINCIPAL SIGHTS.

The following itinerary includes all the most interesting objects, and is the one generally followed by the guides, who give full information on the various points visited. The numbers refer to the position of the places on our plan, and on the official map.

1. THE PORTA MARINA, or ancient sea-gate of Pompeii, is the one by which at present the city is entered. The gate had one entrance for carriages and another for foot-passengers.

2. THE LOCAL MUSEUM is *on the right*. Here are several models and small objects found in the excavations; also several figures in plaster of the bodies found amidst the ruins. The bodies were found encased in ashes. A small hole was made, then the plaster was poured in, and the coating of ashes broken off: the result was a model of the person killed.

Turning down a line on the right brings us to the latest excavations of the eighth region. Some objects of interest were discovered, but perhaps the one which has called forth the largest amount of erudition was a fresco, the subject of which seems identical with the judgment of Solomon. In this mural painting the figures are all pigmies. In the centre is a bench with three judges; kneeling at their feet, in an attitude of prayer, is a woman; further towards the foreground is a butcher's table, and upon it a naked babe, which a man is preparing to kill with a large knife, while beside him stands a second woman with an indifferent air. Soldiers and people close the scene. (See page 20.) This fresco has been removed to the museum at Naples. The house is small, and may have belonged to a Jew; hence the subject of the painting, which as a work of art has no value.

In the vicinity a garden has been laid bare. There are indications

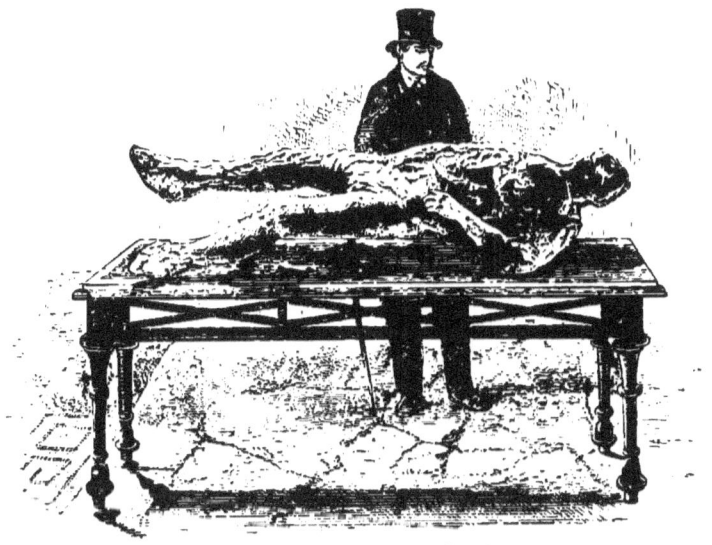

PLASTER CAST OF HUMAN BODY.

of the flower-beds and walks, but the most interesting find was the form of a man encased with what was at the time of his death liquid mud. Plaster of Paris was poured into the space once occupied by the body, and on taking away the volcanic mould it was seen that the man was in the act of fleeing when overtaken in the current. Two keys which he was carrying fell from his hand as it relaxed in the death-throes. He had the usual girdle round his waist, and his loins were girded up to facilitate his flight.

"The skeleton of a woman with a child was discovered at Pompeii in the narrow street which bounds on the north Insula 7 of Regione 8, about twelve feet above the level of the ancient pavement—that is

TEMPLE OF VENUS.

to say, where the layers of lava end and those of ashes begin. It is well known that the catastrophe of 79 A.D. commenced with a thick shower of small pumice-stones, by which the streets and open squares of Pompeii were covered up to the roofs of the houses. Stones were succeeded by ashes, which became solid owing to the action of successive showers of boiling water, and these ashes now form the top layer of the materials which cover the ruins of Pompeii. Most of the unhappy beings who remained in the houses after the eruption first reached the town, and who found, when the shower of stones was over, that no deliverance was possible except in flight, made their escape through the windows, the doors having been blocked by the stones and lava. But, so far as we can judge from the excavations, the greater part of these fugitives could have taken but few steps, and must have been quickly suffocated by the poisonous fumes. The hot ashes and water covered their bodies in such a way as to make an exact cast; and after the flesh had shrunk away, the impression made by the corpses still remains as they fell struck down by death. The Senatore Fiorelli conceived the happy idea of taking plaster casts of the impressions, and thus reproduced the figures to be seen in the Pompeii Museum, which have been copied into most of the books that describe the antiquities of the buried city. It was not always found possible to obtain a perfect cast, because in many instances a portion of the body was resting on the stones, where of course it left no impression. Unfortunately this is the case with the two skeletons lately discovered, the larger of which, that of the woman, is almost entirely embedded in the layer of stones. One arm only has left an impression on the ashes, and with this arm she was clasping the legs of the child, the greater portion of whose body has been modelled, showing considerable contraction in the arms and legs, and a general emaciation; which lead us to suppose that the child must have been very ill. It is believed that it was a little boy about ten years of age. Doubtless the woman was the mother of the child, and we can hardly suppose that she would have carried him had he not been unable to walk. Some jewels found on the female skeleton indicate a person of condition. Two bracelets of gold encircled the arm which held the boy, and on the hand were two gold rings, the one set with an emerald, on which is engraved a horn of plenty, and the other with an amethyst bearing a head of Mercury cut in *intaglio*."

5. THE BASILICA, built of *opus incertum* in bands of brick. This building is not a basilica, but a portico, probably for the same use

THE FORUM.

as the Pœcile Stoa, or painted portico, at Athens; it is a peristylium with no rooms off it. The platform at the end cannot be ascended, and was not a tribunal, but probably dedicated to a divinity: the legs of a bronze statue were found. Basilicæ had flat roofs; this had none. In the open space in front of the columns is the altar. The building is 220 feet long by 80 feet wide, and has nothing in common with a basilica. A graphite or wall-scratch says, "C. Pumidius Dipilus was here on the third of October, in the consulship of Lepidus and Catulus." This gives us the date 79 B.C., and shows the building is older than that. The columns were formed of brick coated over with plaster. Under the platform is a small chamber, miscalled a prison.

6. TEMPLE OF VENUS.—It was surrounded with a Doric portico, which has been changed into an Ionic portico. In the cella stands the pedestal of the statue now in Naples. The altar bears the names of the magistrates who erected it—Marcus Porcius, Lucius Sestilius, with the ædiles Gneius and Aulus Cornelius. The sundial—column to the left in ascending the steps of the temple—was erected by the duumvirs Lucius Sepunius and Marcus Herennius.

The following inscription found here records some repairs and alterations:—

MARCUS HOLCONIUS RUFUS AND CAIUS IGNATUS POSTHUMUS, DECEMVIRS OF JUSTICE THIRD TIME, BY A DECREE OF THE DECURIONS BOUGHT THE RIGHT OF CLOSING THE OPENINGS FOR 3000 SESTERCES, AND ERECTED A WALL AS HIGH AS THE ROOF TO THE COLLEGE OF THE INCORPORATED VENEREI.

On the threshold of the cella—a copy of the original, now in the Naples Museum—are some dots supposed to correspond with Oscan letters, which would read: The Quæstor *Oppius Campanius*, by sanction of the council, permitted *this pavement* to be done by the treasury of Apollo. Hence it is supposed that this temple was dedicated to Apollo. Why not to Apollo and Venus? The statue of Venus, the bronze Apollo, and the oracular Diana, were all found here; and the conical stone, the symbol of the Apollo, as representing the sun, is still to be seen in the cella.

7. THE FORUM, or market-place, is of considerable extent, and was surrounded by a Doric colonnade which supported a balcony. Around were the public offices and temples. There are several frescoes in the Museum at Naples, very badly done, representing various scenes in the Forum.

8. THE TEMPLE OF JUPITER occupies one end of the Forum, from

TEMPLE OF JUPITER.

which it was approached by a flight of steps. This temple was greatly damaged by the earthquake of 63, and was undergoing restoration at the time of the final destruction. From the top there is a fine view over the city.

At either side were arches giving entrance to the Forum. This end of the Forum is shown, after the earthquake, upon an altar in the house of Lucius Cæcilius Jucundus. (See page 67.)

9. THE PANTHEON, or Temple of Augustus. His statue stood in the centre of the court, surrounded with the statues of the twelve great gods. The cells on the right were for the priests. The walls were covered with frescoes. This inscription was found,—

...AMINI . AVGVSTALI . SODALI
AVGVSTALI . Q.

An altar relating to the worship of Augustus, bearing the name of the consuls for A.D. 3, came to light in 1890.

A . A . P . R . D . D
GRATVS . CÆSAR
I . MINIST . IVSSV
Q COTRI . D . V . I . D
C . ANNI . MARVLI
D . ALFIDI . HYPSAL
D . V . V . A . S . P . P
M . SERVILIO . L . ÆLIO
COS

10. THE HALL OF THE TOWN COUNCIL, for the meetings of the city magistrates.

11. TEMPLE OF MERCURY.—In the centre is the marble altar, with a relief representing a sacrifice. It is now used as a depository for small objects found in excavating: many are interesting.

12. CHALCIDICUM OF EUMACHIA, or Guild Hall of the Fullers. Erected by Eumachia the priestess and her son, and dedicated to Concord and Pieta Augusta.

Inscription over entrance to the Chalcidicum from the Street of Abundance,—

EUMACHIA, DAUGHTER OF LUCIUS, PUBLIC PRIESTESS, IN HER NAME AND THAT OF HER SON, M. NUMISTRUS FRONTO, MADE THIS CHALCIDICUM AND CRYPTO-PORTICO AT HER EXPENSE, AND DEDICATED THE SAME TO CONCORD AND PIETA AUGUSTA.

The niches in the front towards the Forum contained statues of Æneas, Romulus, Cæsar, and Augustus, with the following inscriptions:—

TRIANGULAR FORUM AND TEMPLE OF HERCULES.

ÆNEAS, SON OF VENUS AND ANCHISES, BROUGHT TO ITALY THE SURVIVORS OF THE TROJAN WAR. BUILT THE CITY OF LAVINIA, AND REIGNED THERE THREE YEARS. AFTERWARDS, WHEN A BATTLE HAD BEEN FOUGHT, HE VANISHED, AND WAS TAKEN INTO THE NUMBER OF THE GODS.

ROMULUS, THE SON OF MARS, BUILT ROME, AND REIGNED THIRTY-EIGHT YEARS. HE SLEW ACRON, KING OF THE CANENSI, AND DEDICATED THE SPOIL TO JUPITER FERETRIUS. WHEN HE WAS RECEIVED INTO THE NUMBER OF THE GODS HE WAS NAMED QUIRINUS.

13. THE LAW COURTS consist of three halls. The brickwork construction of these halls is the best in Pompeii, and of the time of Nero.

NEW EXCAVATIONS.—Proceeding by the side of the Law Courts, by the Vicolo della Regina, we come to the new excavations at the city limits on this side. The houses are built against the cliff; one is three stories high. In one of the rooms is a large fountain—the walls of the room being frescoed—and above the fountain is a picture of the river-god Sarnus, with a copious stream of water flowing from a vase.

HOUSE OF THE GLADIATORS.—We so name this house because on the threshold are two gladiators in black and white mosaic. The wall at the end of the atrium represents the back-scene of a theatre, with gladiators in various pose. One figure carries a palm-branch, whilst the figure of Wingless Victory is on the left; Fame, blowing her trumpet, being in a balcony on the right. *Return to*

14. STREET OF ABUNDANCE.—So called from the fountain with head and cornucopia. It was one of the principal streets in the city.

31. HOUSE OF HOLCONIUS.—Beautifully decorated, and with a grand peristyle.

18. THE TRIANGULAR FORUM.—So called from its shape; surrounded by a Doric portico of a hundred columns.

THE TEMPLE OF HERCULES occupies the centre, and was approached by a flight of steps. It is considered from its construction to be the oldest temple in the city. *In front* is the Puteal Numerii, erected over the spot where a thunderbolt had fallen, by the magistrate Numerius Trebius.

24. TEMPLE OF ISIS.—Restored after the earthquake of 63 by Popidius Celsinus, a boy of six. (For details of the worship see Bulwer.) Here was found the skeleton of the priest with the axe; also the following inscription :—

NUMERINUS POPIDIUS CELSINUS, SON OF NUMERINUS,—THE TEMPLE OF ISIS HAVING FALLEN FROM AN EARTHQUAKE, RESTORED IT FROM THE FOUNDATIONS AT HIS OWN EXPENSE. THE DECURIONS, ON ACCOUNT OF HIS LIBERALITY, ELECTED HIM, WITHOUT FEES, TO BE ONE OF THEIR ORDER AT THE AGE OF SIX.

The Curia Isiaca is a Doric portico, behind the temple, 79 feet by 57 feet. At the end is a tribunal ascended to by well-worn stairs. Adjoining it are three cells. The name of the builder is recorded in the inscription :—

M. MARCUS HOLCONIUS, SON OF RUFUS THE SWIFT, BUILT THE CRYPT, TRIBUNAL, AND THEATRE AT HIS OWN EXPENSE, FOR THE HONOUR OF THE COLONY.

19. Tragic Theatre, containing twenty-eight tiers of seats. It held 5,000 spectators.

Upon the first step of the second row of seats the inscription informs us there was a bisellium, or chair of honour.

TO MARCUS HOLCONIUS RUFUS, SON OF VIBIUS. FIVE TIMES DUUMVIR, TWO OF THEM QUINQUENNIAL. MILITARY TRIBUNE, ELECTED BY THE PEOPLE. PRIEST OF AUGUSTUS, FATHER OF THE COLONY. ERECTED BY A DECREE OF THE DECURIONS.

Being built against the side of a hill, the people entered at the top, and descended to their seats. It was covered occasionally with an awning for the protection of the audience. The holes which supported the masts can be seen on the outside.

20. Gladiators' Barracks, round a large square with a colonnade all round.

21. Comic Theatre.—The inscription says it was roofed in. It held 1,500 people.

Over door 19 Stabian Street is the inscription,—

CAIUS QUINCTIUS VALGUS, SON OF CAIUS, AND MARCUS PORCIUS, SON OF MARCUS, DUUMVIRS, BY A DECREE OF THE DECURIONS CONTRACTED AND ERECTED THE COVERED THEATRE, AND THE SAME APPROVED IT.

The pavement of the orchestra is of beautiful coloured marble, the name of the donor being inserted in bronze,—

MARCUS OCULATIUS VERUS, SON OF MARCUS, DUUMVIR OF THE GAMES.

The original bronze letters were stolen, and in replacing them they put the name Holconius.

22. Porta Stabiana.—The oldest gate in the walls of Pompeii; constructed with irregular stones from the river Sarnus. The

vaulted arch has been restored. On the outside of the gate is this inscription in Latin,—

AVIANUS AND SPEDIUS, THE DUUMVIRS, PAVED THE ROAD FROM THE MILESTONE TO CISIARII, WHICH WAS ON THE CONFINES OF THE POMPEIAN TERRITORY, AT THEIR OWN EXPENSE.

From here we make a digression out of the usual route to the neighbourhood of the Stabian Gate, to the Leather Manufactory (Officina Coriariorum), adjoining which, and interesting only to some, is

23. THE MASONIC HALL.—From the arrangement of this hall there is no doubt in our minds that here we have preserved an ancient lodge-room. The number of the columns down two sides, the two columns in advance, the position of the pedestal upon which was found the mosaic now in the Naples Museum (see page 13), the small room within the lodge, and scratchings upon the walls, all go to confirm our belief. *Note* certain marks and scratches on the wall of the house in the street. A flight of steps leads from the hall into a garden.

25. SHRINE OF THE BENIGN JUPITER (amiable or propitious).—At the corner of the Via Stabia, No. 25, and the Via Tempio d'Iside, is a small shrine, in which was found the terra-cotta statue of Jupiter now in the Naples Museum. In the small enclosure is a well-preserved altar, and then a flight of steps leading up to the cella. Behind it is the Temple of Isis. Over the inside of the Porta Stabia is an Oscan inscription, being a copy of the original now preserved in the Naples Museum. From it we learn the title of the shrine. It reads:—

THE ÆDILES PUBLIUS SITTUS, SON OF MARCUS, AND NUMERIUS PONTIUS, SON OF PUBLIUS, LAID DOWN THE LIMITS OF THIS STREET, AND FIXED THE TERMINUS OF IT TEN FEET OUTSIDE THE STABIAN GATE. THEY ALSO FIXED THE LIMITS OF THE VIA POMPEIANA [now called Via Stabia] THREE FEET BEFORE THE ENCLOSURE OF JUPITER MELICHIUS. THESE STREETS, AS WELL AS THE JOVIA [Via Amfiteatro] AND DECUMANA [Via Tempio d'Iside], WERE CONSTRUCTED BY THE PUBLIC SLAVES OF POMPEII UNDER THE DIRECTION OF THE SURVEYORS OF THE STREETS, WHICH WAS APPROVED OF BY THE SAME ÆDILES.

27. HOUSE OF CORNELIUS RUFUS, containing his bust and the pedestals of two marble tables.

28. THE AMPHITHEATRE is at some little distance from the present excavations at one corner of the city. It is of the Republican period, contained 12,800 spectators, and is 400 feet long and 114 wide. It had 35 rows of seats. The historian Tacitus ("Annals," xiv. 17) gives us an interesting account of a scene that took place here 59 A.D.:—

THE AMPHITHEATRE, POMPEII.

"About this time a dreadful fray broke out between the inhabitants of Nuceria and Pompeii. Livineius Regulus gave a spectacle of gladiators. An altercation arose, stones were thrown, and finally they had recourse to arms. The people of Pompeii, where the spectacle was given, were too strong for their adversaries. The people of Nuceria suffered in the conflict, and many were conveyed to Rome wounded and mutilated. Many also bewailed the deaths of sons and fathers. The inquiry into this affair was left by Nero to

CAMPANI VICTORIA.

the senate, and by them to the consuls; and on their report upon the merits of the case to the fathers, they punished the Pompeians by forbidding their games for ten years."

The truth of this piece of history has been proved in two different ways.

Scratched on the wall of a house in the Street of Mercury is an armed figure descending the steps of the amphitheatre, bearing in his right hand a palm branch, emblem of victory. Underneath is written,—

CAMPANIANS, YOU PERISH IN VICTORY,
TOGETHER WITH THE NUCERIANS.

And on the walls of a house in the street of Stabia was found a fresco—now removed to the Museum at Naples—representing the amphitheatre with people fighting in and around it, exactly illustrating the above passage in Tacitus. (See page 21.)

There has recently been found outside the Nuceria gate an inscription stating that twenty-two pairs of gladiators, of the priest of Augustus, will fight at Nuceria on the 8th of May, in honour of the power of Augustus.

NVMINI
AVGVSTI
GLAD . PAR . XXII . VENATIO . DAIOMPEI . FLAMINIS . AVGVSTALIS .
PVGNAB . CONSTANT . NVCER . III . PR . NON . NONIS . VIII . EIDVS .
EIDVS . MAIAS .
NVCERINI . OFFICIA . MEA . CERTO . INAI .

27. HOUSE OF EPIDIUS RUFUS, with a handsome atrium and chapel of the household gods.

30. THE STABIAN BATHS.—The oldest baths in the city, used for both men and women. Here we have the complete system of the Roman *thermæ*. These baths are usually entered from the Street of Abundance, and are sometimes called the New Baths.

The inscription preserved in the Museum at Naples records certain restorations :—

CAIUS ULIUS, SON OF CAIUS, AND PUBLIUS ANINIUS, SON OF CAIUS, DUUMVIRS OF JUSTICE, BY A DECREE OF THE DECURIONS CAUSED TO BE ERECTED, WITH THE MONEY WHICH BY LAW THEY WERE TO EXPEND ON THE GAMES OR PUBLIC MONUMENTS, THE LACONICUM [SWEATING-ROOM] AND DESTRICTARIUM [SCRAPING-ROOM], AND RESTORED THE PORTICO AND PALESTRA : WHO APPROVED THE SAME.

We enter the peristylium, formed with fluted Doric columns, which was used as a palæstra for athletic sports. On one side is the Frigidarium, or cold bath, communicating with the Tepidarium, or warm room, and the Apodyterium, or dressing-room. On the opposite side is the Spoliarium, or unrobing-room, with niches and seats, having a fountain at the end. From here we enter the Sudatorium, or sweating-room. Beyond is the Calidarium, or hot bath. These baths are double, being both for men and women. They were highly decorated with frescoes and stucco.

37. HOUSE OF THE BEAR.—So called from the wounded bear represented on the mosaic pavement. He has been transfixed with a spear, which remains in the wound. His blood flows on to the pavement. Over his back is the word HAVE, used as a sign of salutation, from the verb *avere*, to be joyful (Cicero, " Ep. Fam." viii. xvi. 4 ; Martial, " Ep." i. lvi. 6).

40. HOUSE OF MARCUS LUCRETIUS, a flamen of Mars and decurion of Pompeii. In the garden is a fountain down which the water flowed into a circular basin. Around are various animals in marble.

RECENT EXCAVATIONS.

Extensive baths and some houses have been excavated within the last few years on the right of the Street of Nola, turning out of the Stabian Street. The most interesting are the following :—

CASA DEL CENTENARIO.—The House of the Centenary is so called because it was found on the eighteen hundredth anniversary of the destruction of the city. It is one of the most important yet excavated, forming a complete *isola*, or block by itself. It has several entrances. Entering the grand peristylium, we notice the remains of the fountain with its bronze tap. Here was found the beautiful bronze statuette of the Faun now in the Naples Museum. On one of the columns of the peristylium are scratched the letters IIVNVILO. This house, like many others at the time of the destruction of the city, was undergoing repairs—one of the sides of the peristylium being left unfrescoed, the other being finished. In the fountain the remains of fish were found. Off the sides of the inner peristylium are rooms frescoed. One *on the right* has frescoes on a white ground of beasts fighting, and below comical scenes of boys on stilts. Another has a yellow ground with doves and flowers. *On the left* are beautiful frescoes on a black ground; and another small room has Egyptian figures on a white ground, the bottom panels being ferns, acanthus plants, and dog lilies. In the end room are theatrical scenes and a large fresco of Neptune.

The following inscription on one of the street walls advertises an entertainment in the amphitheatre:—

"Twenty pairs of gladiators, at the expense of Decimus Lucretius Satrius Valens, priest, in the consulship of Nero, son of Cæsar Augustus, and ten pairs of gladiators, at the expense of Decimus Lucretius, son of Decimus Valens, will fight at Pompeii on the 10th, 11th, 12th, 13th, and 14th of April. There will be a complete hunting scene, and the awnings will be spread.—Written by Celer. Emilius Celer, the inscription writer, made this by moonlight."

CASA DELLO SPECCHIO.—In another house close by the above are represented the siege of Troy, with men hauling the famous white horse; the story of Perseus and Andromeda; peacocks, etc. In the wall near the entrance is inserted a piece of looking-glass, held to the plaster by four nails. It is discoloured by the action of heat and earth, but its use is obvious.

CASA DELL' ABBONDANZA.—In the same vicinity a house has been uncovered which we will call the House of Abundance, from the statuette in bronze found in a niche entering into the peristylium, and which is now in the Naples Museum. Another bronze statuette was also found here of a Cupid with a dolphin on his shoulder. This served for the fountain in the peristylium. The frescoes here are Ariadne abandoned, and other mythological stories.

We called attention,* soon after its excavation, to a curious piece of architectural detail in the peristylium of this house—in the fact that from the columns of the peristylium arches spring direct from the capitals to support the covered portico which surrounds the court. This style of construction was generally supposed to date from the time of Diocletian (284-305), till we called attention to the fact that it exists here in a house built before A.D. 63.

CASA DELLA FONTANA IN MUSAICO.—Another house close by contains a beautiful fountain in yellow, white, green, and blue mosaic, nautilus pattern, with bands of cockle-shells; whilst around the

* See *The Builder*, July 4, 1881.

walls are all kinds of fish swimming in clear water, and above them are animals fighting, the panels being divided by caryatides.

An excavation made in the presence of the Russian Grand Dukes (1881) brought to light a beautiful fountain in blue mosaic. At the top is the figure of Venus rising out of a shell, deer and leopards drawing cars; whilst at the sides are birds and figures, all exquisitely finished.

On the left of the street a house was excavated in September 1883, and the government have roofed it in, in order to preserve the frescoes *in situ*. *On the right* of the peristylium, in a small frescoed chamber, is a good fresco of Apollo and Venus, with two females attending her. The head of the goddess is curiously reflected in the water. On the opposite side of the court, in another room, is Leda and the Swan.

46. HOUSE OF ORPHEUS.—So called from the fresco. Nearly opposite is the

* HOUSE OF LUCIUS CÆCILIUS JUCUNDUS.—On the threshold is a dog in mosaic—CAVE CANEM. The proprietor was a banker. Scratched on one of the walls is this inscription in Latin : "May he who loves do well. May he who does not know how to love perish. Twice perish he who forbids to love."

In the atrium of the house of Lucius Cæcilius Jucundus the base of a family altar has been found, which is interesting from the buildings sculptured on one of its marble panels, showing the topography of the northern part of the Forum at Pompeii. A triumphal arch, the Temple of Jupiter, with pedestals on each side surmounted by equestrian statues, a flight of steps upon which an altar is burning, a vase upon a *patera*, an altar upon which there is a victim, a female bust beneath a canopy, and a man leading a bull to sacrifice, are represented. These buildings are presented to the view as crooked, and are supposed to refer to the earthquake of 63 A.D., the sacrifices being offered to the gods to appease their wrath. (See pages 58, 8.)

The *tabellæ* or records found in this house have been unrolled and deciphered. A great number have been successfully treated. Great praise is due to the various gentlemen who have by their patience and learning thus preserved these interesting records. (See page 26.)

HOUSE OF THE POETS.—Passing through the house of Jucundus we come to that part of the city which is now being excavated. There is a small niche at the entrance dedicated to Hercules, and containing a representation of that hero in fresco ; a small bronze statuette was also found. Upon the walls of one of the rooms two portraits were found *vis-à-vis* of youthful heads crowned with bay wreaths, with rolls in their hands. On one is a tablet with the name Homer, upon the other Sappho ; they are of course ideal. They have been removed to the Museum at Naples. (See page 21.) There are some glass windows in this house, and quite a modern w.-c.

53. HOUSE OF THE FAUN.—The finest house in Pompeii, in which everything found was classical. It was the house of Arbaces the Egyptian.

55. TEMPLE OF FORTUNE.—Erected by Marcus Tullius in the reign of Augustus. Inside the niche is the inscription—

AVGVSTVS CÆSAR . FATHER OF HIS COUNTRY.

And on the architrave—

MARCUS TULLIUS, SON OF MARCUS, DUUMVIR, QUINQUENNIAL FOR THE THIRD TIME, AUGUR, MILITARY TRIBUNE, ELECTED BY THE PEOPLE, BUILT FROM THE GROUND, AT HIS OWN EXPENSE, THE TEMPLE OF FORTUNE AUGUSTUS.

To the right we pass under the

TRIUMPHAL ARCH OF NERO, formerly cased in marble and surmounted by the bronze equestrian statue now in the Museum at Naples.

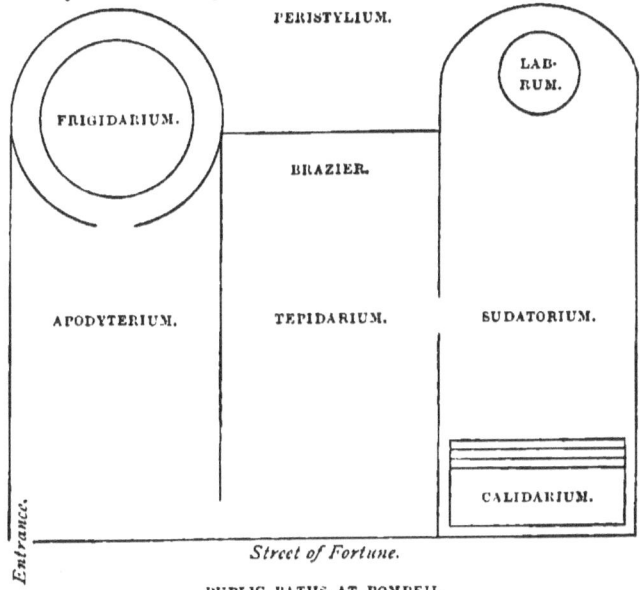

PUBLIC BATHS AT POMPEII.

67. PUBLIC BATHS.—Though rather small, sometimes called the Fortunæ Thermæ, because generally entered from the Street of Fortune.

THE TEPIDARIUM.

A corridor (*fauces*) gives access (*left*) to an open court, surrounded with Doric columns (*peristylium*), used for athletic sports (*palæstræ*). *On the left* is the unrobing chamber (*apodyterium*); the holes in the walls were for the wooden pegs. The walls were frescoed in yellow; the cornice Egyptian in character, with a carved frieze of lyres, dolphins, chimæræ, and vases upon a red ground. The niche at one

THE CALIDARIUM.

end was covered with glass, and held a lamp; above was a glass window, 2 feet 8 inches by 3 feet 8 inches, having one plate of cast glass two-fifths of an inch thick, ground on one side. Beneath is a mask with tritons and dolphins. The floor is white mosaic.

From here we enter the TEPIDARIUM or warm chamber.

In the walls are a number of niches divided by atlases or telamones (from the Greek τῆλναι. to endure) of terra-cotta, painted flesh colour, with black hair and beards. These niches were for the clothes, and frescoed in imitation of porphyry. The vault is in stucco, with low relief of flying genii and foliage, and a red and blue ground. A window, 2 feet 6 inches by 3 feet, held a bronze frame holding four panes of glass. Beneath is a bronze brazier 7 feet by 2 feet 6 inches, having the front legs of winged sphinxes, with lion's paws. In the centre of the front is a cow in relief. Three bronze

THE FRIGIDARIUM.

seats were also found with cows' heads at the top of the legs, and cloven hoofs for the feet. Upon them is the inscription—

M. NIGIDIUS . VACCULAS . P.S.

The cow was evidently his coat-of-arms—a pun upon his name, derived from his ancestors being cowkeepers.

A door leads into the SUDATORIUM or sweating-room, containing at one end the *calidarium* or hot-water bath, and at the opposite end, in an apse, the circular *labrum* or washing-tub. Within it is the bronze inscription—

GNÆUS MELISSÆUS, SON OF GNÆUS APER ; MARCUS STAIUS, SON OF RUFUS, DUUMVIRS FOR THE SECOND TIME, BY DECREE OF THE DECURIONS, MADE THIS LABRUM AT THE PUBLIC EXPENSE. IT COST 750 SESTERCES. [About £6.]

A circular opening 1 foot 6 inches in diameter admitted fresh air through the vault above ; square windows gave light.

From the apodyterium we reach the FRIGIDARIUM or cold plunge bath.

This is a circular chamber with yellow stucco, the vault being a truncated cone frescoed blue, with a window for emitting light. The cornice of red stucco represents chariot races by cupids. The dado is of marble, and the walls are pierced with four niches having seats. In the centre is a depressed basin, 12 feet 10 inches in diameter, and 2 feet 9 inches deep. This was entered by two marble steps. A bronze spout supplied the water, and a waste-pipe carried it off. This was the department for the men ; that for the women adjoins, and is similar in its arrangements. The same set of furnaces supplied both, but there was no communication between the two departments.

These baths were originally erected in the time of P. Sylla, and the construction shows that they were repaired at later dates. There is a scratching on the wall (*right* in entering) of the peristylium referring to the dedication—

ON THE DEDICATION OF THE BATHS, AT THE EXPENSE OF CNÆUS ALLEIUS NIGIDIUS MAIUS, THERE WILL BE A HUNT, ATHLETIC SPORTS, SHOWERING OF PERFUMES, AND AN AWNING (AT THE AMPHITHEATRE). PROSPERITY TO MAIUS, CHIEF OF THE COLONY.

68. HOUSE OF THE TRAGIC POET, or of Glaucus in Bulwer's "Last Days of Pompeii." It once contained some good frescoes, now in the museum at Naples. One of the most elegant houses yet found.

58. HOUSE OF THE LARGE MOSAIC FOUNTAIN.—In the form of an apse. The water poured from the mask down the steps into the basin ; the masks on the sides served for lamps at night.

59. HOUSE OF THE SMALL MOSAIC FOUNTAIN.—The water issued from the swan held by the genius.

69. The HOUSE OF PANSA is a good specimen of a Roman house. He was ædile of the city, and is one of Bulwer's characters. In the

HOUSE OF THE TRAGIC POET.

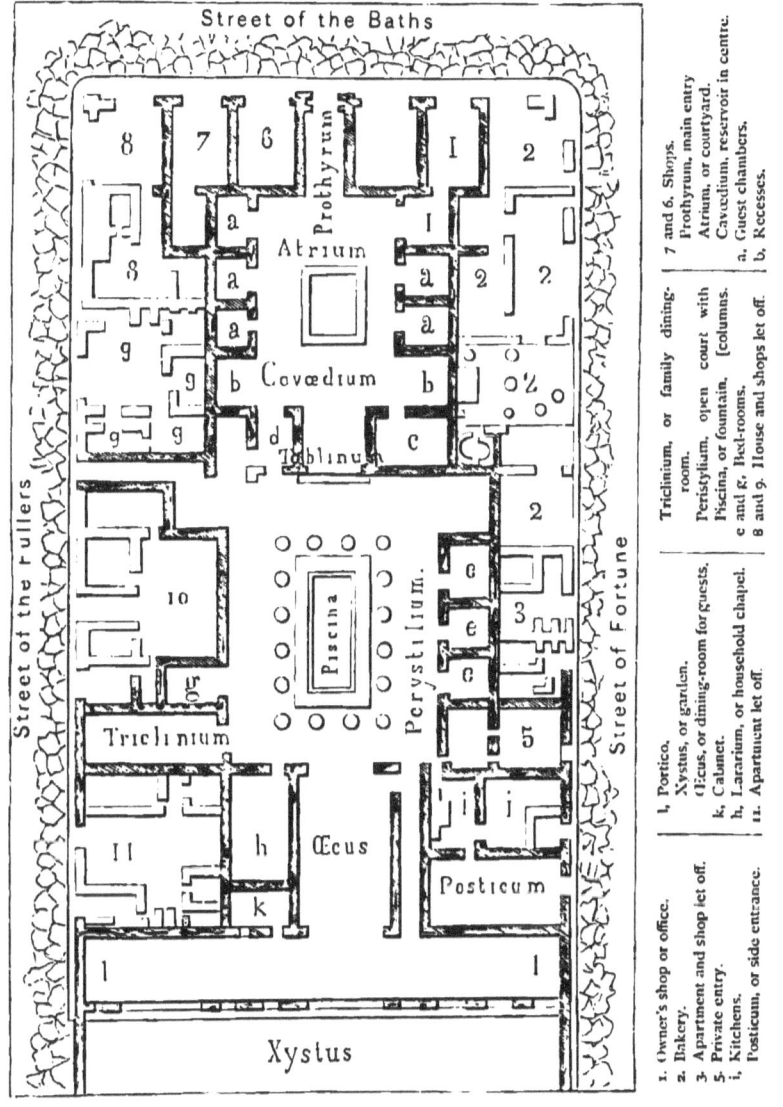

PLAN OF THE HOUSE OF PANSA.

kitchen is a fresco of the worship offered to the Lares. Adjoining are a bakery and mill. Venus's hair now grows in the oven.

This was named the House of Pansa from the graphite PANSAM ÆD. scratched on one of the walls; but further research brought to light an inscription showing that the property belonged to a certain Maius.

TO LET, FOR THE CALENDS OF JULY, SHOPS, WITH THEIR TERRACE, CABINETS, ETC. ADDRESS—PRIMUS, SLAVE OF CNÆUS ALLEIUS NIGIDIUS MAIUS.

In order that our readers may fully understand the arrangement of a Pompeian house of the better sort, we present them with a plan of the House of Pansa, which occupies a block by itself, 300 feet by 100 feet.

STREET OF SALLUST.

STREET OF SALLUST.— From beyond the House of Pansa we enter the Street of Sallust. At its head another street branches off to the

GATE OF HERCULANEUM, POMPEII.

right. The Strada di Sallustio leads to the Gate of Herculaneum and Street of Tombs. Here the polygonal blocks of silex or lava with which the roads were paved can be conveniently examined. They were originally smooth and close-jointed, but have got into their present state by the wear and tear of traffic and the rain washing away the edges of the stones.

72. HOUSE OF SALLUST.—This was evidently the house of a well-to-do man, and is of considerable extent. Most of the frescoes are good in style. Sallust and his house are well known to readers of Bulwer's work.

75. HOUSE OF THE VESTAL VIRGINS, so called, but this is evidently a misnomer. It is composed, in fact, of two houses, the inner one being

THE HOUSE OF IONE.—Visitors will recognize the portico garden and fountains. They are still in good preservation.

78. THE GATE OF HERCULANEUM consists of three arches. The walls, showing construction of various periods, can best be examined at this point. There are some masons' marks here similar to those upon the walls of the Temple of Victory upon the Palatine Hill. (See "Rambles in Rome.")

STREET OF TOMBS.

Walk down on the left side and return by the other. The most interesting tombs are—

79. TOMB OF MAMIA the priestess.

MAMIA, DAUGHTER OF PUBLIUS, PUBLIC PRIESTESS. THIS PLACE OF SEPULTURE WAS GIVEN BY A DECREE OF THE DECURIONS.

82. TOMB OF SCAURUS, upon which are represented gladiatorial combats and wild-beast hunts of the gladiatorial school of Numerius Festus Ampliatus. The names recorded on this tomb are those used by Bulwer in the "Last Days of Pompeii."

The inscriptions read—

TO AULUS UMBRICUS SCAURUS, SON OF AULUS OF THE MENENIA GENS, DUUMVIR. THE DECURIONS DECREED THE SITE OF THE MONUMENT AND 2,000 SESTERCES FOR THE FUNERAL, AND AN EQUESTRIAN STATUE IN THE FORUM OF POMPEII.—SCAURUS THE FATHER TO HIS SON.

83. TOMB OF N.EVOLEIA TYCHE, with a relief of a ship in the act of lowering sail in port, and a bust of Tyche; also a relief of the magis-

STREET OF TOMBS.

trates and family pouring oblations over an altar at the dedication of the tomb.

NÆVOLEIA, FREEDWOMAN OF JULIA TYCHE, FOR HERSELF AND CAIUS MUNATIUS FAUSTUS, AUGUSTAL OF THE SUBURB, TO WHOM THE DECURIONS, WITH THE CONSENT OF THE PEOPLE, DECREED THE BISELLIUM FOR HIS MERITS. THIS MONUMENT NÆVOLEIA TYCHE IN HER LIFE MADE FOR HER FREEDMEN AND FREEDWOMEN, AND THOSE OF CAIUS MUNATIUS FAUSTUS.

84. TOMB OF THE AUGUSTALIS CALVENTIUS, on which is a relief of the Bisellium, or chair of state.

TO CAIUS CALVENTIUS QUINTUS, AUGUSTAL, TO WHOM FOR HIS MUNIFICENCE WAS, BY DECREE OF THE DECURIONS AND WITH THE CONSENT OF THE PEOPLE, GRANTED THE HONOUR OF THE BISELLIUM.

CICERO'S VILLA.—In the neighbourhood of Pompeii Cicero had a villa. He says: "We intended to set sail, Lucullus for his villa near Naples, and I myself towards mine, in the district of Pompeii" ("Academics," ii. 3).

The site has not been discovered, for the villa named after him, on the left outside the Porta Herculanea, was not his. This was excavated many years ago, and the excavation filled in. It belonged to Marcus Crassus Frugius. The mosaics of Dioskorides of Samos and the frescoes of the Bacchantes found here are now in the Naples Museum.

90. VILLA OF DIOMEDES.—Here eighteen bodies of men, women, and children were found in the vaults of the portico, with the remains of food, money, and jewellery. This villa is alluded to by Bulwer.

This extensive villa was built on the plan of a Roman villa as described by Vitruvius. It is of the time of Augustus, and may therefore have been designed by that celebrated architect. On its discovery in 1763 many beautiful mosaics and frescoes were found, but these have been destroyed or removed. Our view presents the large garden surrounded by a portico with a fountain in the centre. At the far end are the apartments of the villa which faced into the garden; and at the higher level behind them was the dwelling consisting of numerous chambers built round a peristylium.

Returning by the opposite side of the road.

85. THE TOMB OF ARRIUS DIOMEDES.

MARCUS ARRIUS, FREEDMAN OF DIOMEDES, TO THE MEMORY OF HIMSELF AND HIS MAGISTRATE OF THE SUBURB, AUGUSTUS FELIX.

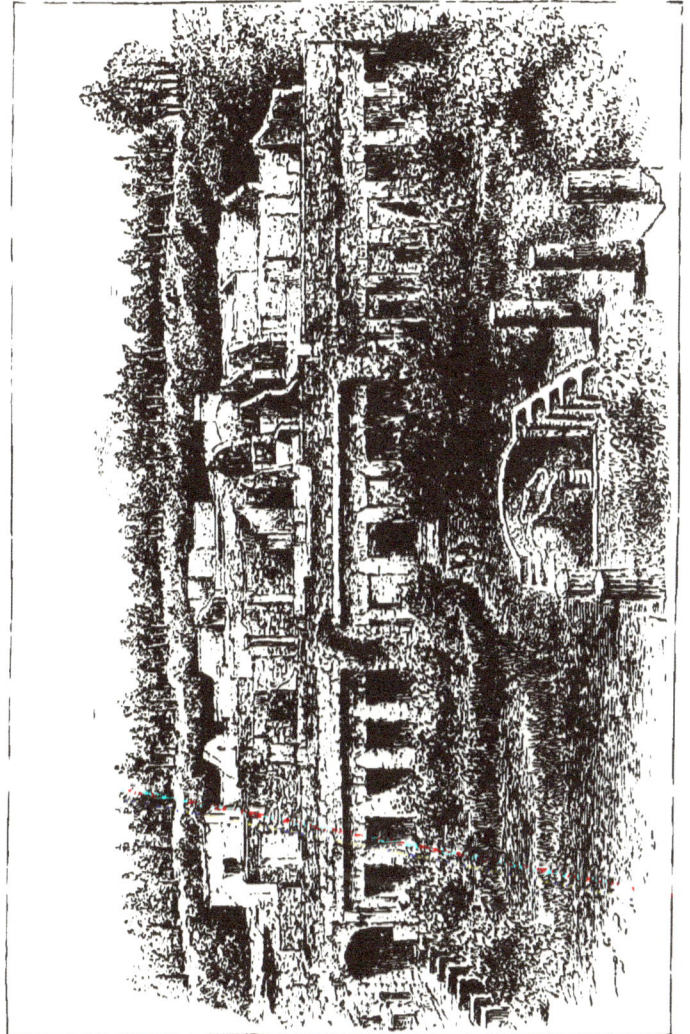

VILLA OF DIOMEDES.

88. TOMB OF LUCIUS LABEON.

TO LUCIUS CAIUS LABEON, SON OF LUCIUS OF THE MENENIA GENS, FOR THE SECOND TIME DUUMVIR QUINQUENNIAL. MENOMACUS THE FREEDMAN ERECTED IT.

86. TOMB OF THE GENS LIBELLA.

TO MARCUS ALLEIUS LUCIUS LIBELLA, THE FATHER, ÆDILE, DUUMVIR, PREFECT QUINQUENNIAL; AND TO MARCUS ALLEIUS LIBELLA, THE SON, DECURION, WHO LIVED SEVENTEEN YEARS.
THE SITE OF THE MONUMENT IS GIVEN BY THE PUBLIC.
ALLEIA DECIMILLA, DAUGHTER OF MARCUS, PUBLIC PRIESTESS OF CERES, MADE THE SEPULCHRE OF HER HUSBAND AND SON.

Then follow a columbaria and an ustrina, or place for burning bodies.

81. Ruins of a VILLA and public-house adjoining. Here were found the four beautiful mosaic columns in the Museum at Naples.

The visitor re-enters the gate, and proceeds through the Forum. When about fifty yards through the arch look back through the arch. We pass out by the sea-gate. For trains consult local time-table.

THE CITY OF THE DEAD: IMPRESSIONS.

On the fifth day of November, eighteen hundred years ago, Vesuvius poured forth streams of fire, liquid mud, ashes, and red-hot stones, thus destroying the cities at its base, and so preserving for after ages a Roman city, that we might know something more of the domestic manners and customs of the Romans than can be learned from books.

On this anniversary we spent the day wandering through and examining the deserted city (with which we are already familiar), partly disentombed from its bed of lava ashes. On the street of Nola the excavations are now being carried out, the latest discovery being a house evidently belonging to a gentleman of the period, who was a bachelor; so at least we should judge from internal evidence. The peristylium with its coloured columns, the marble fountain, and the frescoes on the walls, might well be envied by any bachelor of the Albany. One small fresco struck us with its beauty and subject. Upon a rock in a beautiful landscape sat a youth holding up a lighted lantern; below him was a narrow sheet of water; upon the opposite shore a tower of *opus quadratum*, from a window of which looked out a fair lady, with her arm extended, bearing in her hand a lighted lamp—such as have been found in great numbers amid the surrounding ruins. In the water is seen the form of a manly swimmer, his brow encircled with a laurel wreath. Here we have the story of Leander. From this house it is but a step into the new baths just excavated,—the largest and finest baths in the city, evidently in progress of construction, when the workmen dropped their tools and fled in consternation—never to return.

As we ramble amidst the ruins we have constant evidence that the city was undergoing extensive restorations, and we remember that in 63 it was partly destroyed by an earthquake; and so we know why so much rebuilding was going on when the city was overwhelmed. In one house we see represented upon an altar the end of the Forum with its Temple of Jupiter and arches, as it appeared tottering from the quake. We walk along the silent streets, and note every here and there huge stepping-stones, which must have prevented any horse traffic; then we mark the ruts caused by wheels along the streets and between the stones, and fancy the drivers must have even excelled a "hansom" driver to have steered clear, even if the horse could have stepped over the stones. We know there could not have been much horse traffic in such a city as this, and it is therefore reasonable to suppose that the ruts were caused by hand-barrows and not by chariots. In the wet season the rain rushes along these streets in torrents, and without the stepping-stones the inhabitants could not have crossed dry-shod. We stop and pick up a piece of glass, and the thought strikes us, what misconception exists among many that the Romans knew not of its use for windows. Not only is it mentioned by ancient authors, but here we see it so used. In the baths there is a window 2 feet 8 inches by 3 feet 8 inches, in which was found glass half an inch thick, ground on one side to prevent any one looking into the bath-chamber. In another room was found a bronze frame 2 feet 6 inches by 3 feet, with four panes of clear glass fastened by means of nuts and screws. In the villa of Diomedes four panes were found, 6 inches by four inches; and in a house one is still *in situ*. Glass was then as now used for mosaics, and the art of glass-blowing must have been largely practised, from the numerous specimens existing in different museums. Toughened glass, so lately invented, was discovered, but suppressed by Tiberius putting the inventor to death. As we pass along we notice the leaden water-pipes with their bronze cocks cropping up through the pavement of the side-walks; the water being brought into the city by the aqueducts and stored in the reservoirs, whence it was dispersed by means of leaden pipes to the public fountains, baths, and houses. Another misapprehension exists amongst many, that the Romans, because they built the aqueducts, did not know that water finds its own level, when the aqueducts are built upon that very principle. We mean by this the whole system, not merely a ruined arch, which is all that most visitors see of the Roman water supply.*

STREET OF THE BALCONY.

We stroll into the vacant theatre and note how the people were being amused when the alarm first spread, and see how easily all could get outside the building without crowding or confusion. Why are not theatres built upon this plan now ?

Even the telephone was foreshadowed by these Romans; for, that the voice might reach every part of the house and convey its sound

* See "The Roman Aqueducts and Fountains." By S. Russell Forbes.

to the hardest hearer, little bronze cups were suspended at intervals under the seats of the spectators. What lessons might we not still learn from them, and the arrangement of their houses with their pleasant courts, where the dweller could warm himself in the winter's sun, or shade himself from the summer heats, the sparkling fountain refreshing the air around. Their old custom of letting out part of the ground-floor, facing on to the street, as shops, is still practised by the Italians; and many a prince adds to his income by this means, as well as reserving one for the sale of his own produce. The checkers are still used now as then. Even the houses of the poorer class are nicely if inexpensively frescoed, looking cheerful and comfortable; and, after being buried so long, are far cleaner than many not a thousand miles away. Iron bedsteads and many domestic utensils show that we have not made much progress. In fact, they put more art into ordinary life and things in that easy-going time than we do in this express age.

This city of two miles in circuit impresses one greatly—though visitors are warned not to expect too much, or things on too grand a scale. Fancy you are going to see the ruins of a provincial town of the present day after it has been destroyed by fire; this may give you some idea, but not the correct one. You will say everything seems small; so it may with our present ideas. But think back; remember this was a place of no great importance, that the people passed most of their time out of doors, and were not domesticated like our Anglo-Saxon race. The temples will excel our churches in architecture, and their public buildings ours of the provincial town. Three different baths have been discovered here: where is the provincial town that can show these?—we had almost said one. Stroll into the Forum (market-place). Many of the scenes enacted here are preserved in fresco, giving us a good idea of the original. What town at home has such a market-place? You see you cannot compare the two places; everything is so different,—manners, life, country, and time, all are changed.

There is evidence in the strata of lava ashes that the city was only buried at the great eruption, and that it took many after eruptions to cover it to the depth found. And there is no doubt that many of the houses were entered after the destruction, and that many valuables were carried off. We noticed a rather curious circumstance in this visit. Passing along a short blind street, the pavement was broken away, probably from the giving way of the soil below, leaving a large hole, showing ashes beneath the pavement above, and some feet below the ashes another pavement. Was this a trace of the earlier earthquake or of an earlier unrecorded eruption?

CAMALDOLI.

Visitors to Pompeii who go by the early train can return by the 12.36 p.m. train, so that the afternoon can be spent in an excursion to the Convent of Camaldoli, 5½ miles north-west of Naples.

It was founded by Prince Colonna, and stands on a ridge 1,450 feet above the sea, commanding the most extensive view near Naples. Nothing is more enchanting than this view, taken about an hour before sunset. Below it are the Phlegræan fields; beyond these, to the right, Elysium and the Trumpeters' promontory; to the left the Sirens' town and cape; Naples and its environs occupying the extensive bays between; Circello, Terracina, Gaeta's Bay, and the Apennines filling in the background.

The carriage passes by the Via Roma, and turns just beyond the Museum, by the Via Salvator Rosa and the Via S. Gennaro, to the village of Antignano, where donkeys can be hired for the ascent to the suppressed monastery.

PÆSTUM.

Travellers who wish to see Pæstum, and not Amalfi or Salerno, can stay overnight at Pompeii and take the early train to Pesto, changing at Battipaglia. (See page 130.)

RAMBLE IV.

PORTICI—RESINA—VESUVIUS: HOW TO GET THERE; AND USEFUL HINTS—HISTORICAL NOTICES—HERCULANEUM—LA FAVORITA.

PORTICI.

THE road from Naples is lined with houses and villas till we reach the suburb of Portici, which takes its name from the Porticum Herculis, mentioned by Petronius as standing at the west side of Herculaneum. The highroad passes through the courtyard of the palace of Charles III. We are then in the town of

RESINA,

the ancient Retina, and port of Herculaneum. It is interesting as standing on the top of Herculaneum.

MOUNT VESUVIUS.

Places should be booked overnight at Messrs. Thomas Cook and Son's office, Piazza dei Martiri. Their carriages take passengers to the station at the foot of the cone, from whence the ascent is made by the funicular railway, the property of Mr. John M. Cook. The inclusive cost is 25 lire.

Visitors who do not desire to make the ascent will find it enjoyable to go as far as the Hermitage to view the lava beds.

THE ASCENT OF VESUVIUS BY RAILWAY.

The ascent of Vesuvius has been rendered much easier by the funicular railway which has been made up the steepest part of the cone. Before reaching the Observatory a new road leads off to the right, at the base of the cone, to the station; here the rail is taken, which puts one down within one hundred yards of the summit. The start from Naples is made at 8.30 A.M. in the winter and 7 A.M. in the summer. The trains start running at 10 A.M., and cease at 4 P.M. Special arrangements can be made for night service.

The new station of the railway which ascends to the summit of Vesuvius is situated on a level spot on the west side of the mountain, about half an hour's walk from the Observatory. The constructers of the railway have adopted the American double iron-rope system.

There are two lines of rails, each provided with a carriage divided into two compartments, and capable of holding ten persons. While one carriage goes up the other comes down, thus establishing a counterpoise which considerably economizes the steam of the stationary traction engine. The incline is extremely steep, commencing at 40 degrees, increasing to 63 degrees, and continuing at 50 degrees to the summit. Every possible precaution has been taken against accident, and the railway itself is protected against possible flows of lava by an enormous wall. The ascent is made in eight to ten minutes. To obtain the necessary supply of water, large covered cisterns have been constructed, which in winter are filled with the snow that often falls heavily on Vesuvius. This snow is quickly melted by the internal heat; and besides the water thus obtained, the frequent rainfall is also conducted into the cisterns. An elegant café restaurant, capable of accommodating one hundred persons, is attached to the station. Above the entrance to the latter is an ample terrace supported on columns, whence an enchanting view is obtained, not only of the Gulf of Naples, but also of those of Baiæ and Gaeta, each dotted with its islands, while to the north spreads the luxuriant plain of Caserta, bordered by the distant Apennines.

The funicular railway up to the crater of Vesuvius is in full working order, and is a great success. It is 896 yards long, and the carriages are so constructed that, rising or descending, the passenger sits on a level plane, and whatever emotion or hesitation may be felt on starting, changes, before one has risen 20 yards, into a feeling of perfect security. The motion also is very gentle, and the effect is magnificent, if not, indeed, grandly awful, as, when hanging midway against the side of the cone, one looks from the window directly upwards or downwards along the line, which, its slight incline alone excepted, is perfectly perpendicular. Dismounting at a little station at the summit, one can scarcely be said to clamber to the edge of the crater, for the company have cut a convenient winding path, up which all, except the aged, heavy, or feeble, can walk with ease. For the exceptions the usual helps and chairs can be obtained. The upper station is 3,885 feet above the sea-level, and 1,302 feet above the lower station. The crater is 4,197 feet above the sea. There is a good restaurant at the lower station.

HISTORICAL NOTICES.

The state of Vesuvius is described before the first eruption, A.D. 79, by Florus (iii. 20):—

"Spartacus, Crixus, and Œnomaus, breaking out of the fencing school of Lentulus, escaped from Capua with not more than thirty of the same occupation; and having called the slaves to their standard, and collected a force of more than ten thousand men, were not content with merely having escaped, but were eager to take vengeance on their masters. The first theatre for action that attracted them was Mount Vesuvius. Here, being besieged by Clodius Glaber, they slid down a passage in the hollow part of the mountain, by means of ropes made of vine branches, and penetrated to the very bottom of it; when, issuing forth by an outlet apparently impracticable, they captured, by a sudden attack, the camp of the Roman general, who expected no molestation."

Also by Plutarch in his Life of Crassus:—

"The Romans besieged them in their fort, situated upon a hill that had a very steep and narrow ascent to it, and kept the passage up to them; all the rest of the ground round about it was nothing but high rocks hanging over, and upon them a great store of wild vines. Of these the bondmen cut the strongest strips, and made thereof ladders, like to ship-ladders of ropes, of such a length and so strong that they reached from the top of the hill even to the very bottom. Upon these they all came safely down, saving one that tarried above to throw down their armour after them, who afterwards by the same ladder saved himself last of all. The Romans mistrusting no such matter, these bondmen compassed the hill round, assailed them behind, and put them in such a fear with the sudden onset that they fled every man, and so was their camp taken."

And by Martial (iv. 44):—

> "Here verdant vines o'erspread Vesuvius' sides,
> The generous grape here poured her purple tides;
> This Bacchus loved beyond his native scene;
> Here dancing satyrs joyed to trip the green;
> Far more than Sparta this in Venus' grace;
> And great Alcides once renowned the place:
> Now flaming embers spread dire waste around,
> And gods regret that gods can thus confound."

Also by Strabo (bk. v. iv. 8):—

"Above these places rises Vesuvius, well cultivated and inhabited all round, except its top, which is for the most part level, and entirely barren, ashy to the view, displaying cavernous hollows in cineritious rocks, which look as if they had been eaten in the fire; so that we may suppose this spot to have been a volcano formerly, with burning craters, now extinguished for want of fuel."

VESUVIUS BEFORE THE FIRST ERUPTION.

The great eruption is graphically described by Dion Cassius in his "Life of Titus," bk. lxvi. :—

"During the autumn a great fire broke out in Campania. Vesuvius is a mountain on the coast near Naples, which contains inexhaustible fountains of fire; and formerly it was all of the same height, and fire rose in the middle of it (for the only traces of fire were in the middle), but the outer parts remain unscathed to this day. Hence, these continuing uninjured, but the centre being dried up and reduced to ashes, the encircling crags still retain their ancient height; but the burnt part being consumed, in lapse of time has settled down and become hollow, so that, to compare small things to great, the whole mountain now resembles an amphitheatre. And the tops are clothed with trees and vines; but the circular cavity is abandoned to fire, and by day it sends up smoke, and by night flame, so that one would think all sort of incense vessels were burning there. This continues always with more or less violence, and often, after any considerable subsidence, it casts up ashes and stones, impelled by violent blasts of wind, with a loud noise and roaring, because its breathing-holes are not set close together, but few and concealed.

"Such is Vesuvius, and these things take place in it almost every year. But all eruptions which have happened since, though they may have appeared unusually great to those even who have been accustomed to such sights, would be trifling, even if collected into one, when compared to what occurred at the time of which we speak. Many huge men surpassing human stature, such as the giants are described to have been, appeared wandering in the air and upon the earth, at one time frequenting the mountain, at another the fields and cities in its neighbourhood. Afterwards came great droughts and violent earthquakes, so that the whole plain boiled and bubbled, and the hills leapt, and there were noises under ground like thunder, and above ground like roaring; and the sea made a noise, and the heavens sounded, and then suddenly a mighty crash was heard, as if the mountains were coming together; and first great stones were thrown up to the very summits, then mighty fires and immense smoke, so that the whole air was overshadowed, and the sun entirely hidden, as in an eclipse.

"Thus day was turned into night, and light into darkness; and some thought the giants were rising again (for many phantoms of them were seen in the smoke, and a blast, as if of trumpets, was heard), while others believed that the earth was to return to chaos,

VESUVIUS IN ERUPTION.

or to be consumed by fire. Therefore men fled, some from the houses out into the ways, others that were without into their houses; some quitted the land for the sea, some the sea for the land, being confounded in mind, and thinking every place at a distance safer than where they were. Meanwhile, an inexpressible quantity of dust was blown out, and filled land, sea, and air, which did much other mischief to men, fields, and cattle, and destroyed all the birds and fishes, and besides buried two entire cities, Herculaneum and Pompeii, while the population was sitting in the theatre."

The next eruption was in 203 A.D., in the tenth year of Septimius Severus, as recorded by Dion Cassius: "There appeared at the same time a great fire from Mount Vesuvius, and it made so prodigious a noise that it was heard at Capua, which is the place of my retirement when I am in Italy."

These eruptions seem to have gone on for a series of years. Procopius ("De Bel. Got." iv. 35) thus speaks of Vesuvius at the end of the classic period:—

"Vesuvius is very precipitous below, encircled with wood above, terribly wild and craggy. In the centre of its summit is a very deep chasm, which we may suppose to reach quite to the bottom of the mountain; and it is possible to see fire in it, if a man dare peep over. Usually the fire feeds upon itself (ἐφ' ἑαυτὴν στέφεται), without molesting those who live in its neighbourhood; but when the mountain utters a roaring noise, in general it emits soon after a vast body of cinders."

Numerous accounts have been written of the later displays, the last of which was in 1872. In all these eruptions the villages and towns at the base have been more or less destroyed, and rebuilt only to be again destroyed.

After the descent, a visit can be made to

HERCULANEUM.

("*Herculea Urbs.*"—OVID, "Met." xv. 711.)

The entrance to the excavations is in the Vico di Mare, on the right-hand side of the road, over which are the words "SCAVI DI ERCOLANO." *Admission, 2 lire, including guide. Sundays gratis. By rail, Portici is the station for Herculaneum. Turn to right on exit from station. The direct way is by tram from Naples to Resina.*

This town derived its name from Hercules, and was destroyed at the same time as Pompeii, in the great eruption of A.D. 79. It was discovered in 1719, ninety feet below the present level. It seems to have been destroyed by streams of liquid mud, which, on cooling, hardened into peperino stone, so that the buildings have had to be quarried out; hence little has been done in comparison with Pompeii.

HISTORICAL NOTICES.

"Hercules built a small town of the same name as himself in the place where his fleet lay at anchor, which, being now inhabited by the Romans, and lying in the midway between Pompeii and Naples, has at all times a secure harbour" (Dionysius, i. 44).

"Herculaneum, built upon a promontory which projects out into the sea, and which, on account of the prevalence of the south-west wind, is a very healthy spot" (Strabo, v. iv. 8).

"Which fortified hill, on the sea, defended with low walls, between two rivers, is within a short distance of Vesuvius" (Sisenna, quoted by Nonius Marcellus, viii.).

"One part of it was ruined by an earthquake during the consulship of Memmius Regulus and Virginius Rufus," A.D. 63 (Seneca, "Q. N." vi.).

There is evidence, as at Pompeii, that considerable restorations were going on at the time of the final catastrophe.

Livy (x. 45) records the taking of Herculaneum, and its being added to Rome, by Carvilius, consul A.U.C. 459.

"Carvilius had in the meantime taken from the Samnites Volana, Palumbinum, and Herculaneum. At Herculaneum, it is true, the consul had two regular engagements without any decisive result on either side, and with greater loss than was suffered by the enemy; but afterwards, encamping on the spot, he shut them up within their works, besieged and took the town."

Velleius Paterculus (ii. 16) tells us that Herculaneum was taken by his ancestor for the Romans in the Italian War (80 B.C.):—

"Minatius Magius of Æculanum, my ancestor in the fourth degree, grandson of Decius Magius, displayed in this war such a faithful attachment to the Romans, that he, in conjunction with Titus Didius, took Herculaneum, and with Lucius Sylla besieged Pompeii."

"Lycurgus had taken us to a feast in honour of Hercules, which was held in a little town in the neighbourhood; but having heard we were there, they followed in all haste, and met us in the portico of the temple" (Petronius Arbiter, ii.).

This temple was found in the original excavations, its marbles and works of art carried off, and the excavation filled in.

"This was the place renowned by the divinity of Hercules. All now lies buried in flames and sad ashes" (Martial, iv. 44).

THE THEATRE.

The following inscriptions were found here on fragments of the cornice which decorated the entries :—

A MAMMI RVFVS . IIVIR . QVN. THEATR.

ORCH DE . SVO

and—

L. ANNIVS . L. F. MAMMIANVS . RVFVS . IIVIR

QVINQ . THEATR . O P. NVMISIVS.

P. F. AR TEC.

A brick stamp was also found with the words,—

ABDAE . LIVIAE.

These show that the Theatre was built by Annius Mammianus Rufus, in the time of Augustus, and that Publius Numisius was the architect.

A flight of dark steps descends to the Theatre, containing 19 tiers of seats, which, with the stage and orchestra, is all that can be made out. It held 10,000 people, and is one of the largest ancient theatres remaining.

After returning from the Theatre, the guide conducts you to the other excavations, SCAVI NUOVI, in the Vicolo di Mare. Here some houses and streets have been excavated. One called the House of Argus and Io, from the fresco, is enclosed in an arcade, and in another trees are growing in the ancient peristylium.

Cavaliere Novi, a retired officer, who has devoted himself to the study of archæology, has lately been so fortunate as to discover, in the vicinity of Herculaneum, the ruins of immense thermæ and various other edifices adjoining. They are still covered by more than 30 feet of volcanic matter from Vesuvius, and about 18 feet of the lava of 1631. Competent persons who have visited the spot agree in declaring that the construction of these baths is admirable, and that nothing similar exists in the neighbourhood. As soon as permission is obtained, excavations on a large scale will be commenced; and it is expected that many valuable objects will be found, for the part of the building already uncovered proves that it belongs to the best period of Roman art.

Three quarters of a mile beyond Resina is

LA FAVORITA,

a royal villa with beautiful gardens and views. *Permission—see Directory at end of Rambles.*

RAMBLE V.

GROTTO OF POSILIPO—GROTTA DI CANE—LAGO D'AGNANO—ASTRONI—SOLFATARA—POZZUOLI—PAUL'S LANDING-PLACE—BRIDGE OF CALIGULA—TEMPLES OF SERAPIS, NEPTUNE, AND THE NYMPHS—CICERO'S VILLA—THEATRE—AMPHITHEATRE—MONTE NUOVO—ARCO FELICE—CUMAE—GROTTO OF THE SIBYL—GROTTA DELLA PACE—LAKES AVERNUS AND LUCRINUS—TEMPLE OF APOLLO—GROTTA D'AVERNO—VIA HERCULEA—STUFE DI TRITONI—BATHS OF NERO—BAIAE—TEMPLES OF DIANA, VENUS, AND MERCURY—LAKE FUSARO—AGRIPPINA'S TOMB—BACOLI—VILLA BAULI—CENTO CAMERELLE—PISCINA MIRABILIS—CAPO MISENO—ELYSIAN FIELDS—ISLAND OF NISIDA—GROTTO OF SEJANUS—VILLAS OF POLLIO AND LUCULLUS—SCHOOL OF VIRGIL.

It will be necessary to start at 7.30 a.m. Carriages should be ordered overnight. Pair horse, 25 lire; one horse, 17 lire. Lunch should be taken, or can be had at Baiæ. A steam tramway now runs to Pozzuoli. (See page 141.)

A railway has been opened from Naples, station at Montesanto, off the Via Roma, by Pozzuoli, Arco Felice, and Baja to Torregaveta, on Cape Misenum, from whence steamers run to the islands of Procida and Ischia, about 13 miles. It is handy for going to Pozzuoli and Baiæ, but not for making the excursion to Cumæ. A stop-over can be made at Pozzuoli and another train taken on to Baiæ.

The best way to make this complete excursion is by carriage; but should time be limited, go as far as Pozzuoli by the steam tram or by the train, and hire a carriage there.

THE GROTTO OF POSILIPO.

The hill of Posilipo took its name from the villa of Vedius Pollio, called Pausilypum (end of care). Through the hill is cut the cele-

THE GROTTO OF POSILIPO.

brated Grotto, evidently as a means of communication instead of going over the hill. To the left above the entrance is Virgil's tomb. This tunnel of the Romans will compare favourably with some of our railway tunnels, and was made for the same purpose. Traces of its ancient lining (*opus reticulatum*) still remain. It is 757 yards long, 21 to 32 feet wide, 20 to 50 feet high, and is lighted with gas and two shafts made by Alfonso of Aragon. The ancient tunnel is closed as dangerous, and a new one has been opened on its right. Emerging from the tunnel, we pass the village Fuori Grotta.

After a little, beyond the village, the road turns off to the right, then to the right again, through a deep cutting, to

THE GROTTA DI CANE.

(*Dog's Grotto.*)

Admission, half-lira each. For dog experiment, one lira extra.

Called by Pliny (ii. 93) "the breathing-place of Pluto; infernal vents." It is the custom here to send in a dog, to see how soon he will be stupified by the sulphur—hence its present name. Near it are the STUFE DI SAN GERMANO, where they collect the sulphur. *Entrance, half-lira.* They are on the banks of the drained (1870)

LAGO D'AGNANO,

supposed to be the celebrated fish-pond of Lucullus (Pliny, ix. 54).

At the far end of the valley is a yellow house, on the hill of ASTRONI, now a royal hunting-ground, but formerly a volcano.

To the right is the hill of Camaldoli. (See page 87.)

N.B.—*Turning back, we cross the road by which we came. To the right it goes to the Solfatara; but as the road is impracticable for carriages, and rather long for pedestrians, we advise those who wish to see it to go as far as Pozzuoli in their carriage, and then turning to the right before entering the gate of the town, the carriage will take them within ten minutes' walk of the Solfatara, straight on over rather a rough, steep road. It is not worth the time, trouble, or expense; and as there is so much of interest to be seen on this Ramble, we advise travellers to omit it.*

THE SOLFATARA.

Admission, half-lira each.

It is the crater of an extinct volcano, called by Strabo (v. iv. 6) the Forum Vulcani. "A plain surrounded with hills which seem to be on fire, having in many parts mouths emitting smoke, frequently accompanied by a terrible rumbling noise; the plain itself is full of drifted sulphur." Vapours and gases ascend from the fissures in the soil. Petronius Arbiter ("Carm. de Bell. Civ." xiv.) thus describes it:—

> "A place there is,
> Betwixt Dicarchis and fair Naples town,
> Sunk deep into the gaping ground beneath,
> And watered by the streams of hell, for thence
> The blasts that breathe with deadly heat are charged.
> Green autumn blooms not there; no verdant turf,
> No herbage decks the soil; nor in the spring
> Do the soft shrubs, with discord musical,
> Hold murmuring converse with the gentle breeze:
> But chaos there, and hopeless barrenness,
> Dark rocks, and funeral cypresses are found.
> In this drear spot grim Pluto from the ground
> Reared his dire form, while played around his head,
> With smouldering ashes strewed, sepulchral fires"

Visitors who have gone to the Solfatara will return as far as the Roman road to the right, turning down which, on the right, inside some red gates, is the Amphitheatre. From here they will work backwards. (See page 106.)

After leaving Lago d'Agnano we drive towards the sea. Reaching the village of Bagnoli, where there are some mineral baths, and skirting along the shore, Via Puteolana or Via Antiniana, we pass the quarries worked by convicts. Here is a fine view seaward; to the left the island of Nisida (see page 115), and to the right the cape of Miseno.

BY RAILWAY.

The Naples, Pozzuoli, and Cumæ railway has its terminus in Naples, at Montesanto, off the Piazza Carita. There is also a station on the Corso Vittorio Emanuele, which is convenient to the hotels. (*See local time-tables.*) A long tunnel connects the two Naples stations. The line then runs through a tunnel under the hill of Posilipo, and emerges at Fuorigrotta. Passing through a series of vineyards, it reaches the Terme at Bagnoli. There is a fine view of the island of Nisida (page 115) on the left. It skirts along the shore of the bay and through several tunnels to Pozzuoli, the station there being at the public gardens. Just beyond, it passes by the Temple of Serapis, on the left (page 104). There is a fine view of the cathedral, town, and the ancient landing-place, which has recently been partly rebuilt as a breakwater. The train passes by the Armstrong works, and we get a good view of the castle and bay of Baiæ, with Cape Misenum (page 115). On the right are Monte Nuovo and Lake

Lucrinus. It crosses the causeway of the Via Herculea, and by the so-called Temple of Diana, on the right, runs through a tunnel under the hill and comes out at Lake Fusaro, noted for its oysters (page 114). At the end of the lake it terminates at the slight ruins of the Villa of Vatia, Torregaveta. From here there is a service of boats to the island of Ischia, which looms up out of the sea in front.

It is an hour's run from end to end of the line, and is worth doing, if only for the views, by any who cannot devote a day to this charming excursion.

POZZUOLI,

the ancient Puteoli. "The ancient town of Puteoli obtained from Nero the privilege of a colony and an appellation derived from him-

MOLE OF PUTEOLI.

self" (Tacitus, "Ann." xiv. 27). Its cathedral is on the site of the Temple of Augustus, erected by L. Calpurnius; six of the Corinthian columns are still *in situ*. On the quay are the remains of the ancient mole, sixteen arches still remaining. It was the landing-place from the East. "Titus arrived first at Rhegium, and sailing thence in a merchant ship to Puteoli, went to Rome with all possible expedition" (Suetonius, "Titus," v.). Here Paul landed from the good ship *Castor and Pollux*, and tarried on his journey to Rome : " Where we found brethren, and were desired to tarry with them seven days" (Acts xxviii. 14).

"Dicæarchia was formerly nothing but a naval station of the Cumæi. It was built on an eminence. But at the time of the war with Hannibal, the Romans established a colony there, and changed its name to Puteoli, an appellation derived from its wells, or, according to others, from the stench of its waters" (Strabo, v. iv. 6).

From here Caligula threw a temporary bridge across the bay to Baiæ.

THE BRIDGE OF CALIGULA.

"He invented, besides, a new kind of spectacle, such as had never been heard of before; for he made a bridge of about three miles and a half in length, from Baiæ to the mole of Puteoli, collecting trading vessels from all quarters, mooring them in two rows by their anchors, and spreading earth upon them to form a viaduct, after the fashion of the Appian Way. This bridge he crossed and recrossed for two days together: the first day, mounted on a horse richly caparisoned, wearing on his head a crown of oak leaves, and armed with a battle-axe, a Spanish buckler, and a sword, and in a cloak made of cloth of gold ; the day following, in the habit of a charioteer, standing in a chariot drawn by two high-bred horses, having with him a young boy, Darius by name, one of the Parthian hostages, with a cohort of the Prætorian guards attending him, and a party of his friends in cars of Gaulish make. Most people, I know, are of opinion that this bridge was designed by Caius, in imitation of Xerxes, who, to the astonishment of the world, laid a bridge over the Hellespont, which is somewhat narrower than the distance betwixt Baiæ and Puteoli. Others, however, thought that he did it to strike terror in Germany and Britain, which he was upon the point of invading, by the fame of some prodigious work. But for myself, when I was a boy I heard my grandfather say that the reason assigned by some courtiers, who were in habits of the greatest intimacy with him, was this : When Tiberius was in some anxiety about the nomination of a successor, and rather inclined to pitch upon his grandson, Thransyllus the astrologer had assured him 'that Caius would no more be emperor than he would ride on horseback across the Gulf of Baiæ'" (Suetonius, "Caligula," xix.).

"And other pranks he did like a madman ; as when he laid a

bridge from the city Dicæarchia, which belongs to Campania, to Misenum, another city upon the seaside, from one promontory to another, of the length of thirty furlongs, as measured over the sea. And this was done because he esteemed it to be a tedious thing to row over in a small ship, and thought withal that it became him to make that bridge, as he was lord of the sea, and might oblige it to give marks of obedience as well as the earth; so he enclosed the whole bay within his bridge, and drove his chariot over it, and thought that as he was a god it was fit for him to travel over such roads as this was" (Josephus, "Antiq." xix. i. 1).

At the farther end of the town is

THE SERAPEUM,

(*Fee, half-lira,*)

or Temple of Serapis, consisting of a court enclosed with columns, having thirty-two adjoining chambers. Three Corinthian columns supporting the frieze still remain. The centre of the court was occupied by a circular temple, the sixteen African columns of which are now at Caserta, and the statue of Serapis is now in the National Museum. Inscriptions mention Marcus Aurelius and Septimius Severus as restorers of this temple. The different changes in the level of the water and coast here are remarkable, also the manner in which shell-fish have eaten away the bases of the columns.

THE TEMPLES OF NEPTUNE AND THE NYMPHS

are just beyond. Some columns and fragments rising out of the sea have been dignified with these names.

A little further along the shore, on the cliff to the right, some fragments mark the site of

CICERO'S PUTEOLANEUM VILLA,

which Cicero called his Academy, and where his "De Fato" and part of the "Academica" were composed. (See "Cicero's Letters to Atticus.")

"Travelling from Puteoli towards Lake Avernus, it is to be seen on the sea-shore, renowned for its fine portico and its grove. Cicero gave it (the grove) the name of Academia, after the grove so called at Athens. It was here that he composed those treatises of his that were called after it; it was here, too, that he raised those monuments to himself, as though, indeed, he had not already done so throughout the length and breadth of the known world. Shortly after the death of Cicero, and when owned by Antistius Vetus, hot springs burst

TEMPLE OF SERAPIS.

forth at the very front of the house, which were beneficial for the eyes, and have been celebrated in verse by Laurea Tullius. I will give the lines, as they deserve to be read, not only here but everywhere,—

> ' Great prince of Roman eloquence, the grove
> Which thou didst raise is verdant now,
> Thy walk, from the Academy named,
> From Vetus now its finished graces takes.
> Here now streams burst forth, unknown before,
> Which with their spray the languid eye relieve.
> Thy land, I ween, these bounteous springs revealed
> To honour Cicero, its ancient lord.
> Throughout the world his works by eyes are read—
> May eyes unnumbered by these founts be healed!'"
>
> —(Pliny, xxxi. 2)

Spartianus ("Hadrianus," xxv.) says Hadrian died at Baiæ, and was buried in this villa; and here Antoninus Pius founded a temple to him (*Ibid.* xxvii.).

HADRIAN TO HIS SOUL.

"Animula vagula blandula
Hospes comesque corporis,
Quae nunc abibis in loca
Pallidula, rigida, nudula,
Nec, ut soles, dabis jocos?"

[Guest and companion of my breast,
Tender, wandering little soul,
Pallid, naked, cool,
Not given, as thy wont, to jest,—
To what place at length departing?]

Such were the words addressed by the emperor, as he lay on his death-bed, to his departing spirit. He had lived an active life, and as old age and disease crept on him he wished to die. He seems to have suffered greatly, and Dion Cassius tells us that he made great complaints of his sickness and the misery he was reduced to in not being able to die himself, although he could put others to death. Spartianus records his death and the above words, which he repeated just before he expired.

These words of Hadrian's inspired our English poet Pope, who composed the following lines on this subject:—

"O fleeting spirit, wandering fire,
That long hast warmed my tender breast.
Wilt thou no more my frame inspire,
No more a pleasing, cheerful guest?
Whither, ah! whither art thou flying,
To what dark, undiscovered shore?
Thou seem'st all trembling, shivering, dying,
And wit and humour are no more."

From the Serapeum a steep road lined with trees leads to the back of the town, where is the Amphitheatre. In a vineyard on the right are some ruins of

THE THEATRE.

Two rows of arches, some corridors and vaults, are all that remain.

"Augustus corrected the confusion and disorder with which the spectators took their seats at the public games, after an affront which was offered to a senator at Puteoli, for whom, in a crowded theatre, no one would make room. He therefore procured a decree of the senate, that in all public spectacles of any sort, and in any place whatever, the first tier of benches should be left empty for the accommodation of senators" (Suetonius, "Augustus," xliv.).

In the opposite vineyard are the ruins of some baths, now called the Temple of Diana, and a reservoir near is called the Temple of Neptune, and another reservoir the Labyrinth.

Numerous ruins are scattered about the hill, but they are not of much interest.

THE AMPHITHEATRE.

Admission, one lira.

There were four tiers of seats, and the principal entrances had triple colonnades. Black Corinthian columns mark the emperor's seat. The arena is 369 feet by 216, and underneath are the passages and dens for the beasts. It held 35,000 people. It was here that Nero gave Tiridates his grand entertainment described by Dion Cassius: "At Puteoli he gave him the diversion of a combat of gladiators. Patrobius, his freedman, had the care of it, and made an expense so extraordinary that in a whole day there was nothing seen upon the Amphitheatre but men, women, and children of Ethiopia, in which this Patrobius seems to be worthy of praise. Tiridates shot at the beasts from his throne, and it is said that at one shot with his bow he killed two bulls."

Round the arena are the spaces of the trap-doors, reached from the basement by means of lifts or elevators, and through which men and beasts sprang upon the stage.

Descending the hill, we pass on the left several tombs. Our road— the ancient Via Cumana—leads round the bay, of which we have a fine view, also the best view of the Moles Puteolanae on our right.

Our road now turns off to the right (but see N.B., page 104), *with*

MONTE NUOVO

on the left, which was upheaved on September 30, 1538, from the midst of Lake Lucrinus. It is 456 feet high. *On our right is* Monte Gaurus or Barbaro.

"If Gaurus, his pinnacles rooted up, were to fall down to the very depths of stagnant Avernus" (Lucan, "Phars." ii. 665).

A short drive brings us to

ARCO FELICE,

a lofty arch of brickwork, evidently for carrying an aqueduct across the gully. It is 63 feet high and 18½ wide. Good view from top.

Following the road to

CUMÆ.

The first settlement of the Greeks in Italy can now boast only a few uncertain ruins. Here dwelt the celebrated Sibyl, who sold her books to Tarquin the Proud; here died the last of the Tarquins, whose tomb existed near the Arco Felice in Petrarch's day. There is an amphitheatre, *to the left of the road before reaching the site of the ancient town*, with 21 tiers of seats.

Remains of the Acropolis and city walls still exist, also slight fragments of temples called the Giants, Diana, and Apollo.

Juvenal (ii. 9) describes the desolation of Cumæ in his time,—

> "The graceful works of art, the sculptured tomb,
> And all the sacred dust that rests beneath,
> In one vast ruin lie....
> And do we grieve if our allotted day
> So swiftly flies, when Fate's destructive hand
> Proud cities sweeps with violence away?
> Nor thou who, on thy seven famed hills enthroned,
> Sitt'st like a sceptred queen, shalt be eternal!
> Nor thou, her rival, in the Hadrian wave!
> And thee, my native city—thee the plough
> (Ah! who could e'er believe?) shall one day raze,
> While the rough swain that guides it, sighing, cries,
> 'She too has had her day of glory!'"

"Cumæ, the most ancient settlement of the Chalcidenses and Cumæans, is the oldest of all the Greek cities in Sicily or Italy (founded 1250 B.C.). At first this city was highly prosperous, as well as the Phlegræan plain, which mythology has made the scene of the adventures of the giants, for no other reason, as it appears, than because the fertility of the country had given rise to battles for its possession. Some are of opinion that Cumæ was so called from τὰ κύματα, the waves, the sea-coast near it being rocky and exposed" (Strabo, v. iv. 4). *Below the rock of the castle is*

THE GROTTO OF THE SIBYL.

"And the Sibyl,—you know I saw her myself at Cumæ with my own eyes, hanging in a jar; and when the boys asked her, 'What would you, Sibyl?' she answered, 'I would die'" (Petronius Arbiter, vii.).

> "A spacious cave, within its farmost parts,
> Was hewed and fashioned by laborious art
> Through the hill's hollow sides: before the place
> An hundred doors an hundred entries grace;
> As many voices issue, and the sound
> Of Sibyl's words as many times rebound."
> VIRGIL, "Æneid," vi. 42.

Returning, before reaching the Arco Felice an ancient road turns off to the right to the Tunnel of Cumæ, or

GROTTA DELLA PACE,

so called from the original explorer. Mentioned by Strabo (v. iv. 5). *Admission for carriage, one lira.* It is supposed to have been made by Agrippa for direct communication between Cumæ and

LAKE AVERNUS,

which is 2 miles round and 210 feet deep. It was the scene of the entrance to the infernal regions of the poets Homer ("Odyssey," xi.), Virgil ("Æneid," vi. 237), and Dante ("Inferno"). No bird would live near it.

> "Bane of the feathered race, its sulphurous womb
> Shot forth foul-steaming poison ; black with gloom,
> And shagged with dismal woods, the tribes around
> Revered it with religion's awe profound."
> SILIUS ITALICUS, xii. 121.

But the same author says later on,—

> "I may now celebrate thee among pleasant lakes."

This was when the waters of

LAKE LUCRINUS

were let into it, the whole forming the Portus Julius. "Augustus formed the Julian harbour at Baiæ by letting the sea into the Lucrine and Avernian lakes" (Suetonius, "Augustus," xvi.). Here Agrippina landed after the attempt on her life. "By swimming, and then meeting with some small barks, she reached the Lake Lucrinus, and was thence conducted to her own villa" (Tacitus, "Ann." xiv. 5). "I am detained by the voluptuous waters of the attractive Lucrine Lake, and the caves warmed with fountains issuing from the rocks of pumice-stone" (Martial, iv. 57).

It was famous for its oysters, and was nearly destroyed by the upheaval of 1538. Pliny (ix. 8) tells a curious story of an attachment between a boy and a dolphin. The fish, on the call of the lad, used to come to him, and carry him on its back to Puteoli to school, and back again.

On the borders of Lake Avernus is a conspicuous ruin called the TEMPLE OF APOLLO, but in fact the extensive remains of thermæ. Towards the end of the lake are numerous caverns cut into the tufa rock. one of which is called the

GROTTA D'AVERNO,

(Fee, 1 lira each; torch, 1 lira each. Guides are extortionists. Carriages can go through.)

and by some the Grotto of the Sibyl, which has an entrance of brick, and is a long, damp channel with vertical apertures. It led from Avernus to Lucrinus. It is 285 yards long. *Beyond* the entrance, a small square chamber is called the Entrance to the Inferno. Near it are remains of a warm bath, with a natural spring called the Bath of the Sibyl. It is entered by mounting the back of the guide, as the mosaic pavement is covered with water from the spring oozing out of the rock.

> "Deep was the cave, and downward as it went
> From the wide mouth, a rocky, rough descent;
> And here th' access a gloomy grove defends,
> And here th' unnavigable lake extends."
> VIRGIL, ".Eneid," vi. 237.

"Agrippa cut a subterranean passage from Avernus to Cumæ. Cocceius, the engineer, fancied that it was natural to this place that its roads should be made under ground" (Strabo, v. iv. 5).

We now come upon the small sheet of water that represents LAKE LUCRINUS, and *turning to the right*, rejoin the road from Puzzuoli.

N.B.—Travellers whose time is limited can omit Cumæ, the tunnels, and Lake Avernus, and instead of turning off at Monte Nuovo, keep straight on to Lake Lucrinus.

The causeway dividing the sea from Lucrinus was called the

VIA HERCULEA.

"This, they say, was constructed by Hercules when he drove away the oxen of Geryon" (Strabo, v. iv. 6). "While enjoying yourself, Cynthia, in Central Baiæ, where extends the path made by Hercules to the shore, and while admiring, now the bay at the foot of the realm of Thesprotus, now that near noble Misenum, does any thought of me prompt you in remembrance?" (Propertius, "El." i. xi.) "Where the lake, shut out from the shady shores of Avernus, dashes up to the smoky ponds of the hot water of Baiæ; and where Misenus, the Trojan trumpeter, lies buried on the shore, and the causeway, built by the labour of Hercules, re-echoes with the waves" (Propertius, iv. 18).

It was afterwards restored by Fabius Maximus after an earthquake.

FABIVS . MAXIMVS . V. C. RECT. PROV.
F....S. PR. VIAS . HERCVLIS . OB.
TERRAE . MOTVS . EVERSAS.
RESTITVIT . A. FVNDAMENTIS.
GRUTER, cl. 9.

After passing the Via Herculea, on the right are remains of some baths called LE STUFE DI TRITONI, *and above them the*

STUFE DI NERONE,

(Baths of Nero,) still the resort of invalids.

"Fair Baiæ's shores, for tepid springs renowned,
Where all the gay delights of life are found."
STATIUS, "Sil." iii. v. 95.

It consists of a long passage cut in the tufa rock, and leading into a chamber where there are several springs 182° F. They are used for rheumatism.

"Quid Nerone pejus?
Quid thermis melius Neronianis?"
MARTIAL, vii. 34.

A short distance on, a new road leads over the hills to Cumæ; beyond, a few houses and ruins mark the site of

BAIÆ.

Albergo della Regina: fair place for lunch.

"Herod and Fortunatus both sailed to Dicæarchia, and found Caius at Baiæ, which is itself a little city of Campania, at the distance of about five furlongs from Dicæarchia. There are in that place royal palaces, with sumptuous apartments, every emperor still endeavouring to outdo his predecessor's magnificence. The place also affords warm baths, that spring out of the ground of their own accord, which are of advantage for the recovery of the health of those that make use of them, and, besides, they minister to men's luxury also" (Josephus, "Antiq." xviii. vii. 2).

"Nothing in the world can be compared with the lovely Bay of Baiæ" (Horace, "Ep." i. 85). Now there is but a fishing village. The whole shore was occupied with the villas and baths of the luxurious Romans. Now the ruins can be scarcely made out, some standing on the shore, others in the sea.

"And though the waves indignant roar,
Forward you urge the Baiæn shore,
While earth's too narrow bounds in vain
Your guilty progress would restrain."
HORACE, "Odes," ii 18.

BAY OF BAIÆ.

"Nowhere do mineral waters abound in greater number, or offer a greater variety of medicinal properties, than in the Gulf of Baiæ, some being impregnated with sulphur, some with alum, some with salt, some with nitre, and some with bitumen, while others are a mixture of quality, partly acid and partly salt. The springs at Baiæ, now known as Posidian, after the name of a freedman of the Emperor Claudius, had waters so hot as to cook articles of food even" (Pliny, xxxi. 2).

It was a favourite resort of Nero's. "Whither the emperor, charmed with the loveliness of the place, was in the habit of going, and where he entered the bath and banquet without his guards, and unencumbered by the pomp of his imperial state" (Tacitus, "Ann." xv. 52).

"Why mention Baiæ, and the shores covered with sails, and the waters which send forth the smoke from the warm sulphur?" (Ovid, "Ars Am." i. 255.)

"While Cærellia, the mother of a family, was sailing from Bauli to Baiæ, she perished by the malice of the raging flood. What glory have ye lost, ye waters! Such a monstrous catastrophe ye did not of old allow to Nero, even though commanded to do so" (Martial, iv. 63).

"Alexander Severus made an imperial palace at Baiæ, with a lake which to this day is named Mammæ, from his mother; and he made in other ways at Baiæ magnificent works in his own honour, and stupendous lakes, admitting the sea" (Lampridius, xxvi. 28).

"They say that Baiæ took its name from Baius, one of the companions of Ulysses" (Strabo, v. iv. 6).

TEMPLES OF DIANA, MERCURY, AND VENUS.

Such are the names given to the three principal ruins. That of Diana is an octagonal building on the outside, and circular in the interior, having four recesses in the walls. That of Mercury is a circular building, with an opening in the vault like the Pantheon at Rome. Curious echo here. That of Venus is similar to Diana's, with remains of lateral chambers, windows, and stairs. All three, from their construction and remains, were no doubt connected with some great thermæ. In that of Venus there are remains of stucco ornamentation. These ruins are parts of baths.

Martial (xi. 80) says,—

> "Land of Venus, golden coast,
> Nature's fairest gift and boast,
> Happy Baiæ."

Visitors should climb to the top of the hill behind Baiæ. Here is a fine panoramic view of the Gulf of Gaeta. Below us is the

LAKE OF FUSARO,

the Palus Acherusia of the poets, formerly the port of Cumae, with two communications with the sea. The Casino is a royal hunting-box. *To the right*, the Arx of Cumae, and *to the left* is the point Torre di Gaveta, the site of the villa of Servilius Vatia, who retired there from public life during the reign of Nero.

Beyond Baiæ, passing the sixteenth century castle of Don Pedro de Toledo, are remains called

AGRIPPINA'S TOMB,
(*Sepolcro di Agrippina,*)

a semicircular passage, with vaulted roof, reliefs, and frescoes, being really the ruins of a theatre. Her tomb was probably further on. Tacitus ("Ann." xiv. 9) says: "She received a humble monument upon the road to Misenum, near a villa of Cæsar, the dictator, which, elevated above the surrounding objects, overlooks the coast and bays below."

"There is something awful and terrific in the sound of the trumpet heard on the neighbouring hills, and in the nightly lamentations supposed to issue from the tomb of Agrippina" (*Ibid.* 10).

Beyond the village of BACOLI, so named from the Villa Bauli, where Nero murdered his mother (see Suetonius, "Nero," xxxiv.), are some remains called the CENTO CAMERELLE, or the Labyrinth, probably the substructions of the VILLA OF JULIUS CÆSAR. "He conducted her to Bauli—so the villa is called—which, lying between Cape Misenum and the Gulf of Baiæ, is washed by the winding sea" (Tacitus, "Ann." xiv. 4). This villa belonged to Hortensius (Cicero, "Academica," ii. 3).

Cicero tells us (ii. 3) that the second of the academic questions was discussed at this villa, and he (26) describes the scene from it:—

"I can see the Cumæan villa of Catulus from this place, but not his villa near Pompeii; not that there is any obstacle interposed, but my eyesight cannot extend so far. What a superb view! We see Puteoli, but we do not see our friend Avianus, though he may perhaps be walking in the portico of Neptune."

"At Bauli, near Baiæ, Hortensius had some fish preserves, in which there was a muræna, to which he became so much attached as to be supposed to have wept on hearing of its death. In the same villa

Antonia, wife of Drusus, placed earrings on a muræna to which she had become attached" (Pliny, ix. 81).

Above this is the

PISCINA MIRABILIS,

(*Fee, half-lira each,*)

a large vaulted reservoir, supported by 48 columns in a good state of preservation; 234 feet long by 88 wide.

"He began a reservoir from Misenum to Lake Avernus, covered in and enclosed by porticoes, into which all the warm springs of Baiæ were to be turned" (Suetonius, "Nero," xxxi.).

"Nero exerted all his might to perforate the mountains adjoining Avernus, and to this day there remain traces of his abortive project" (Tacitus, "Ann." xv. 42).

From the top of the hill we look down upon the ancient harbour of Misenum. The cape beyond is

THE PROMONTORY OF MISENUM,

and was so called after Misenus, the trumpeter of Æneas, who was drowned in the sea below, and buried on this cape. From it there is an extensive view.

> "But good Æneas ordered o'er the shore
> A stately tomb, whose top a trumpet bore,
> A soldier's falchion, and a seaman's oar.
> Thus was his friend interred; and deathless fame
> Still to the lofty cape consigns his name."
> VIRGIL, vi. 232.

Here was the villa where Tiberius died. "And after much shifting of places, he settled at length at the promontory of Misenum, in a villa of which Lucullus was once lord" (Tacitus, "Ann." vi. 50). On the shore below dwelt Pliny, and amidst these hills and shores were the poetical ELYSIAN FIELDS.

In returning, after passing Puzzuoli, take the new road to Naples— Strada Nuova di Posilipo—which leads along the bay, thus obtaining, to the left, a beautiful view of the valley, and to the right, of the

ISLAND OF NISIDA,

now used as a sanitorium, but formerly the villa of a son of Lucullus (Cicero), where Brutus retired after the murder of Cæsar, and where Cicero visited him.

> "And the wood that crowns
> The Nesian isle, deep rooted in the main."
> STATIUS, "Sil." iii. i. 147.

"With such an exhalation does Nisida send forth the Stygian air from its clouded rocks" (Lucan, "Phars." vi. 89).

After passing the little village of Bagnoli, a bend in the road brings us to the so-called

GROTTO OF SEJANUS.

Fee, one lira. Carriages should be left at the entrance, and told to wait; or, better still, for fair walkers, instructed to go on and wait at the Villa Sans Souci on the Naples Road.

This tunnel was evidently cut through the mountain by Lucullus as an easy communication between his villa and the bay of Puzzuoli. The construction—*opus reticulatum*—shows it to be of his time; and as it only led to his villa, it was made for private, not public, convenience. In 1840 it was cleared out and repaired, as a public monument of ancient engineering skill, when an inscription is said to have been found, recording some repairs made by Honorius (400 A.D.). It is 920 yards long. Strabo (v. iv. 5) says: "It was cut by M. Cocceius Nerva" (37 B.C.). Seneca says: "Nothing can be more tedious than this prison-like passage, nothing more gloomy than the entrance, from the villa, which enables us to see the darkness, but not to see through it"—a description which is still faithful. Strabo (v. iv. 7) says: "There is a subterranean passage, similar to that at Cumae, extending for many stadia along the mountain, between Dicaearchia and Neapolis. It is sufficiently broad to let carriages pass each other, and light is admitted from the surface of the mountain by means of numerous apertures cut through a great depth."

On emerging into the vineyard, a slight climb brings us to the ruins of

THE VILLA OF LUCULLUS,

and formerly of Vedius Pollio, consisting of the slight remains of a small theatre and the seats of a larger one, the stage of which has disappeared.

"Pausilypum—from the Greek παυσιλυπον (end of care)—is the name of a villa in Campania, not far from Naples. Here, as we learn from the works of M. Annaeus Seneca, a fish is known to have died sixty years after it had been placed in the preserves of Caesar (so called because left to Augustus, and handed down to his successors) by Vedius Pollio, while others of the same kind, and its equals in age, were living at the time that he wrote" (Pliny, ix. 78).

"Vedius Pollio caused such slaves as had been condemned by him to be thrown into preserves filled with muraenae" (Pliny, ix. 39).

"Lucullus had a mountain pierced near Naples, at a greater outlay even than had been expended on his villa; and here he formed a channel, and admitted the sea to his preserves" (Pliny, ix. 80).

The remains of the dwelling on the promontory beyond are called the

SCHOOL OF VIRGIL,

(*Scuola di Virgilio,*)

as it is said he wrote some of his works here. It is now a confused mass of picturesque ruins.

A walk through the vineyard brings us out into the Naples Road at the Villa Sans Souci, or visitors can return through the tunnel, according as to how they have ordered their carriage.

Emerging into the road, a pleasant drive or walk along the cliffs may be enjoyed, with the sea at our feet, Naples and Vesuvius before us. Pursuing our way, *on the right* some reticulated work marks the site of an ancient villa of the time of Hadrian, now a restaurant. Beyond is the ruined Villa of Donn' Anna, commenced in 1555 by the beautiful niece of Pope Paul IV., Anna Caraffa, but never completed.

RAMBLE VI.

ISLAND OF CAPRI—HISTORICAL NOTICES—BLUE GROTTO—VILLAS OF TIBERIUS—SOR RENTO—CASTELLAMARE—VIETRI—AMALFI—SALERNO—PÆSTUM.

(Four days; or by omitting Amalfi, three days; or omitting Pæstum, two days.)

THE ISLAND OF CAPRI.

The steamboat leaves Naples from St. Lucia between 8 and 9 a.m. Office, 34 Strada Molo Piccolo. Fare, 10 lire; embarkation and landing, 30 centesimi each. Do not go if the wind is east or north, as you cannot then enter the Blue Grotto.

The island of Capri is 1,980 feet above the sea, and is noted for its scenery and as being the residence of Tiberius.

"Capreæ is an island disjoined from the point of the cape of Surrentum by a channel of three miles. I am strongly inclined to believe that Tiberius was taken with its perfect solitude. The temperature of the climate is mild in winter, from the shelter of a mountain, which intercepts the rigour of the winds. Its summers are refreshed by westerly winds, and are rendered delightful from the wide expanse of sea which the island commands" (Tacitus, "Ann." iv. 67).

"At a distance of eight miles from Surrentum is Capri, famous for the Villas of Tiberius. The island is eleven miles in circumference" (Pliny, iii. 12).

THE BAY OF NAPLES.

It is only from the deck of a vessel that one can have any idea of the beautiful situation enjoyed by Naples and its surrounding towns. The shore, the white buildings, the purple hills behind and

ISLAND OF CAPRI.

the blue sky above (perhaps tinted by the smoke from Vesuvius), and the deep blue sea, all go to make up an unequalled picture.

THE BLUE GROTTO.
(Grotta Azzurra.)

Boat from landing-place for one to three people, 1½ to 3 lire. Entrance to the Grotto, 1.25 each. Time, two hours.

Passing the slight remains of the Baths of Tiberius, we arrive at the entrance of the grotto, which being only 3 feet high, visitors must recline in the boat. The height of the interior is 41 feet, with 8 fathoms of water. Length, 175 feet; breadth, 100 feet. The blue reflection completely blinds the visitor at first; and objects in the water have a silvery appearance. The boatman will plunge in, if you wish, for a lira; but it is quite a treat to jump in oneself. The blueness is caused by the reflection of light.

The morning steamer stops at the Blue Grotto, and then proceeds to the Grand Marina landing. Lunch at Restaurant de la Grotte Bleue. For visitors intending to make a stay, *lunch should be had at Stanford's Hotel du Louvre, and bed ordered for the night. After lunch start off, with a boy as guide, for the*

VILLAS OF TIBERIUS.

The ascent is first made to the *Punta Tragàra*, where a capital view of the island may be had.

The hill *Lo Capo* is supposed to be the site of the VILLA JOVIS; and the SALTO DI TIBERIO is the precipice whence the victims were thrown into the sea. The VILLA OF TIBERIUS, beyond, consists of a number of chambers and galleries. Near by are the remains of a LIGHT-HOUSE, from whence there is a good view. Beyond is the VAL DI MITROMANIA with its *natural arch;* and the GROTTO OF MITHRAS, the Persian sun-god, which cavern is entered by a flight of 130 steps. The TUORO GRANDE are the ruins of another villa.

"Tiberius chose for his retreat twelve villas, having different names, and of considerable magnitude" (Tacitus, "Ann." iv. 67).

These villas were probably named after the Dii Consentes, as Suetonius ("Tiberius," lxv.) says that he never stirred out of one of them, the Villa Jovis, for nine months.

Capri and Anacapri are the only towns on the island. Near the latter is DAMECUTA, another imperial villa. The hill *Monte Solaro*, 1,980 feet, can be ascended by good walkers, and a most commanding and enjoyable view will well repay the fatigue.

THE BLUE GROTTO.

HISTORICAL NOTICES.

"In the island of Capri, some decayed branches of an old ilex, which hung drooping to the ground, recovered themselves upon his (Augustus') arrival, at which he was so delighted that he made an exchange with the Republic of Naples of the island of Ischia for that of Capri" (Suetonius, "Augustus," xcii.).

"He spent four days at Capri, where he gave himself up entirely to repose and relaxation." "He likewise constantly attended to see the boys perform their exercises, according to an ancient custom still continued at Capri" (*Ibid.*, xcviii.).

"After Tiberius had gone round Campania, and dedicated the Capitol at Capua and a temple of Augustus at Nola, he retired to Capri, being greatly delighted with the island, because it was accessible only by a narrow beach, being on all sides surrounded with rugged cliffs of a stupendous height and by a deep sea" (*Ibid.*, "Tiberius," xl. See also xliii. and xliv.).

"A few days after his arrival at Capri, a fisherman coming up to him unexpectedly, when he was desirous of privacy, and presenting him with a large mullet, he ordered the man's face to be scrubbed with the fish, being terrified at the thought of his having been able to creep upon him from the back of the island over such rugged and steep rocks. The man, while undergoing the punishment, expressing his joy that he had not likewise offered him a large crab which he had also taken, he ordered his face to be further lacerated with its claws. He put to death one of the Prætorian guards for having stolen a peacock out of his orchard. In one of his journeys, his litter being obstructed by some bushes, he ordered the officer whose duty it was to ride on and examine the road, a centurion of the first cohort, to be laid on his face upon the ground and scourged almost to death" (*Ibid.*, lx.).

"The place of execution is still shown at Capri, where he ordered those who were condemned to die, after long and exquisite tortures, to be thrown before his eyes from a precipice into the sea. There a party of soldiers belonging to the fleet waited for them, and broke their bones with poles and oars, lest they should have any life left in them" (*Ibid.*, lxii.).

"A few days after he died, the light-house at Capri was thrown down by an earthquake" (*Ibid.*, lxxiv.).

N.B.—*Before going to bed, engage a place in the postal boat, Barca Postale, of Michele Desiderio for Sorrento. It leaves early; inquire the time. Fare, 2 lire.*

SORRENTO.

Those not desiring to sleep at Capri can go on to Sorrento by the steamer in the afternoon.

SORRENTO

is celebrated as the birth-place of Tasso (1554), for its mosaic wood-work, and its position. The walks round are interesting, and command good views. There is nothing to see in the town itself. The walls of Surrentum (its ancient name) have long since disappeared; and other slight fragments magnified with the names Amphitheatre, Temple of Neptune, Villa of Pollius Felix, are of little interest.

Tasso's statue now ornaments the principal street, and his house is an hotel (Hotel Tasso).

About a mile and a half out of the town, off the Massa road, is the *Vigna Sersale* (fee, 50 c.). From this site a truly enchanting panoramic view may be enjoyed.

A delightful excursion, in fine weather, is by carriage to Meta and over the hills to Positano, then by the cliff road to Projano, whence by boat (about one hour) to Amalfi.

Take lunch at the Hotel Tramontano, and order a carriage for Castellamare. One horse, 4 lire; 2 horses, 7 lire, inclusive.

THE DRIVE

from Sorrento to Castellamare *is said to be* one of the most beautiful in Europe, amidst orange and lemon groves, mulberry trees, and vineyards; aloes, figs, olives, and pomegranates at every turn; skirting under mountains and crossing ravines, passing picturesque villages and villas. This drive is best done from Sorrento to Castellamare, *not* Castellamare to Sorrento. We consider that it is overestimated.

On leaving Sorrento, a deep ravine is crossed by a bridge. Visitors should descend into this chine, which forms part of the Villa de Angelis. It is not only the most picturesque glen in this neighbourhood, but its natural formation is one of Nature's greatest wonders.

We pass through the villages of Meta and Marina di Seiano. The latter has a picturesque martello tower. These towers were so called from the bells hung in these sixteenth century watch-towers, which, being struck with a hammer (*martello*), gave warning in times of danger to the inhabitants. From this is derived the name of the old round fortified towers on the English coast—martello towers. The next village is Vico Equense.

On the *Punta di Sorrento*, on the road to Castellamare, there is

CASTELLAMARE DI STABIA.

a natural arch and cove called the Bagni della Regina Joanna. Another beautiful view.

This *Piano* was formerly, as now, celebrated for its wines.

"He who skilfully mixes the Surrentine wine with Falernian lees collects the sediment with a pigeon's egg; because the yolk sinks to the bottom, taking down with it all the heterogeneous parts" (Horace, "Sat." ii. iv. 55).

"And the hills robed with generous Surrentine."
OVID, "Met." xv. 709.

"Do you drink Surrentine? Choose for it neither painted myrrhine jars nor vessels of gold; the wine will furnish you with cups from its own locality" (Martial, xiii. 110).

"Accept these cups, formed of no common clay, but the polished work of a Surrentine potter's wheel" (*Ibid.*, xiv. 102).

On arriving, quarters for the night should be taken at the Hotel Quisisana, on the hill.

CASTELLAMARE DI STABIA

is so called from occupying the site of Stabia, which was destroyed by Sylla. Pliny says that in his time "it had dwindled into a villa." It was here that he lost his life, as recorded above. It is a resort for sea-bathing in the summer. The villa and wood of Quisisana, Monte Coppola, and Monte Sant' Angelo, are delightful country excursions.

The early train should be taken to Vietri, changing on to the main line at Torre Annunziati. Beyond Pompeii is VALE DI POMPEII, where a new church has recently been erected to a supposed miraculous figure of the Madonna. It has a very fine organ with sixty stops, which is played by a blind man. Beyond is Nocera, the town that was at enmity with Pompeii (see page 66). Hugo de Pagani, the founder of the order of the Knights Templars, was born here. The citadel was the scene of many dark deeds, and in it Urban VI. was besieged by Charles of Durazzo, whom he had made King of Naples. During the siege the Pope tortured seven of his cardinals, amongst others Adam Hereford, the Bishop of London. Five of them he tied up in sacks and threw overboard on his voyage to Genoa.

On the right of the road, beyond Nocera, is the village and church of S. MARIA MAGGIORE. The church was once a circular temple, its vaulted roof being supported by two rows of twenty-

AMALFI.

eight columns each. In the centre is an octagonal bapistery. Beyond, on the right, is LA CAVA TIRRENI, a pleasant summer resort, and a handy place to make the excursions from to those who have plenty of time. *Hotel de Londres.* It was a favourite place with Salvator Rosa, and is noted for the Benedictine monastery, La Trinita, which contains an immense library of parchment and paper manuscripts. The rail here descends the picturesque valley to VIETRI, from whence we take carriage, by a very beautiful route, to

AMALFI.

Proceed to the Hotel Cappuccini, formerly a monastery, and enjoying extensive views. Amalfi had a bishop in the sixth century, and in the ninth Leo IV. gave it the title of "Defender of the Faith." It rose to be the rival of Genoa and Pisa, with a population of 50,000. An earthquake and storm in 1343 A.D. ruined it, so that now it is only a pleasantly situated town of 8,000 inhabitants, who manufacture macaroni, soap, and paper.

The hotel was founded as a monastery in 1212 A.D., and its cloisters are a good specimen of that period. The town is at the entrance of a deep ravine surrounded with mountains. The principal object of interest is the cathedral (eleventh century). It is dedicated to St. Andrew, whose relics are shown. The front has seven antique columns from Pæstum. The bronze doors are Byzantine, and bear two inscriptions in silver. In the interior are two ancient sarcophagi and a porphyry urn. The choir is composed of ancient columns and mosaics from Pæstum. *Notice* the statue of St. Andrew, and the cloisters.

The bell-tower was erected in 1276 A.D. by the Archbishop Filippo Augustariccio. It has three stories square and a fourth round, surmounted by a cupola with towers at the corners.

It is believed in Amalfi that a native of the town, Flavio Gioja, invented the mariner's compass in 1302 A.D. We do not believe it. St. Luke says he went with St. Paul to Syracuse "and fetched a compass"!

We drive to Salerno in the evening, so that we may see the cathedral in the morning before leaving for Pæstum. *Hotel Victoria.*

SALERNO,

the ancient Salernum, is situated on a beautiful bay, and has a pleasant promenade in the Corso Garibaldi. The cathedral was founded in 1084 A.D. by Robert Guiscard, and dedicated to St.

TEMPLE OF CERES, PÆSTUM.

Matthew. The Norman chief plundered Pæstum for the material, the marble columns of the atrium being from different temples, whilst they used the ancient sarcophagi for their tombs. The bronze doors, originally inlaid with silver, were made by Landolfo Butromile in 1099 A.D. Over the door inside is a mosaic of St. Matthew.

In the right transept is the monument of Gregory VII. (Hildebrand), who died at Salerno in 1085 A.D., a fugitive from Rome. At the end of the nave are the ambos—that on the right supported by twelve granite columns, that on the left by four of black porphyry. They are said to have been made by Giovanni da Procida, 1260 A.D., as also was the mosaic above the tomb of Gregory. In the left aisle is the tomb of Margaret of Anjou.

The chapel of the sacristy has an altar of sculptured ivory—fifty-four scriptural subjects—1200 A.D. From the right aisle we reach the subterranean church, decorated with Florentine mosaics, 1616 A.D. Below the altar are preserved the relics of St. Matthew, said to have been brought from the East in 930 A.D.

The early train should be taken from Salerno to Pesto; change carriages at the Battipaglia junction. There is ample time to see the temples and to lunch, returning to Naples by the afternoon train.

On leaving the station we enter the city by one of the ancient gates (Siren's), and following the path by the Villa Bellelle come upon the highroad, and unexpectedly behold the most impressive sight of three temples, comparatively perfect, standing in a deserted plain. The right-hand temple is called Ceres, the centre one Neptune, and the left one Castor and Pollux. This latter is not a temple, but a basilica.

PÆSTUM.

Lunch should be taken.

The road is not very interesting, and there are no traces of the rose-gardens mentioned by the poets, though violets still abound. " I have seen the rose-gardens of scented Pæstum, that seemed likely to live, fall scorched beneath a morning's south wind" (Propertius, v. 5).

The principal objects of interest are the three Greek temples, considered to be the finest remains out of Greece.

Pæstum was founded by the Greeks, 600 B.C., and took its name from the Phenician of Neptune, Posetan, thence the Greek Posidonia—Pæstum—Neptune's city.

TEMPLE OF NEPTUNE, PÆSTUM.

"The first temple which presents itself to the traveller from Naples is the smallest. It consists of six pillars at each end, and thirteen at each side, counting the angular pillars in both directions. The architrave is entire, as is the pediment at the west end, excepting the corner stones and triglyphs, which are fallen, and the first cornice (that immediately over the frieze), which is worn away. At the east end, the middle of the pediment, with much of the frieze and cornice, remains; the north-east corner is likely to fall in a very short time.* The *cella* occupied more than one-third of the length, and had a portico of two rows of columns, the shafts and capitals of

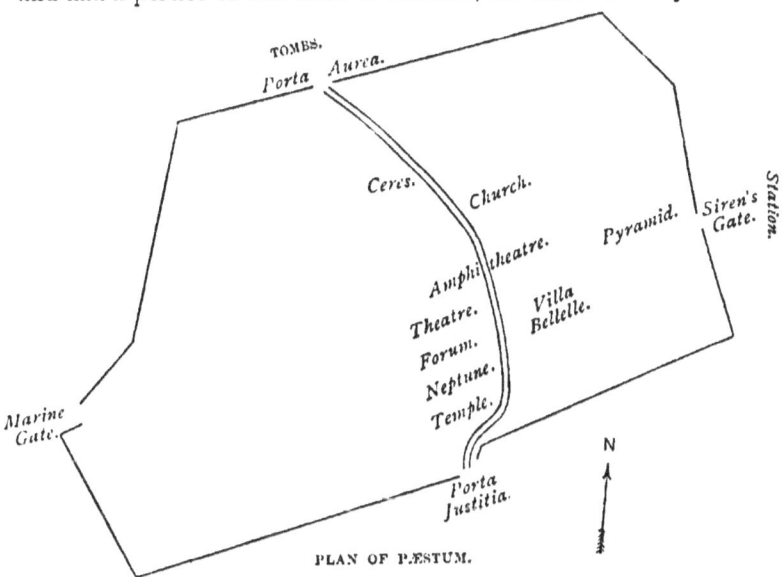

PLAN OF PÆSTUM.

which, now overgrown with grass and weeds, encumber the pavement and almost fill the area of the temple." This is supposed to be the temple of Ceres.

"The second temple has six columns at each end, and fourteen on each side, including those of the angles; the whole entablature and pediments are entire. A double row of columns adorned the interior of the *cella*, and supported each another row of small pillars; the uppermost is separated from the lower by an architrave only, without frieze or cornice. Of the latter, seven remain standing on each side; of the former, five on one side and three on the other. This

* Now restored.

double story, which seems intended merely to support the roof, rises only a few feet higher than the external cornice, and on the whole produces no good effect, from the great disproportion between the under and upper columns. The *cella* had two entrances, one at each end, with a portico formed of two pillars and two *antæ*. The whole of the foundation and part of the wall of this *cella* still remain; under it was a vault. One of the columns, with its capital at the west end, has been struck with lightning, and shattered so as to threaten ruin if not speedily repaired. Its fall will be an irreparable loss, and disfigure one of the most perfect monuments now in existence. It might indeed be restored to its original form with little expense and labour, as the stones that have fallen remain in heaps within its enclosure."* This is called the Temple of Neptune.

"The city of Posidonia, which is built about the middle of the gulf, is called Pæstum. The Sybarites, when they founded the city, built the fortifications close up to the sea; but the inhabitants removed higher up. In after time (442 B.C.) the Leucani seized upon the city, but they in turn were deprived of it by the Romans (274 B.C.). It is rendered unhealthy by a river (Salso) which overflows the marshy districts in the neighbourhood" (Strabo, v. iv. 13). "The Leucani are of Samnite origin. Having vanquished the Posidoniates and their allies, they took possession of their cities" (*Ibid.*, vi. i. 3).

"The third edifice is the largest. It has nine pillars at the ends and eighteen on the sides, including the angular columns as before. Its size is not its only distinction: a row of pillars, extending from the middle pillar at one end to the middle pillar at the other, divides it into two equal parts, and is considered as a proof that it was not a temple. Its destination has not been ascertained; some suppose it to have been a curia, others a basilica, and others a mere market or exchange. In the centre there seems to have been an aperture in the pavement, leading, it is said, to vaults and passages under ground. There is indeed at some distance a similar aperture, like the mouth of a well, which, as our guides informed us, had been examined, and was probably intended to give air and light to a long and intricate subterranean gallery, which extended to the sea on one side, and on the other communicated with the temples." This was probably a temple to the two divinities Castor and Pollux; hence the columns down the centre.

"Such are the peculiar features of each of the edifices. In com-

* Now restored.

mon to all, it may be observed that they are raised upon substructions forming three gradations (for they cannot be termed steps, as they are much too high for the purpose), intended solely to give due elevation and relievo to the superstructure; that the columns in all rise without bases from the uppermost of these degrees; that these columns are all fluted, between four and five diameters in height, and taper as they ascend, about one-fourth; that the capitals are all very flat and prominent; that the intercolumniation is a little more than one diameter; that the order and ornaments are in all the same, and the pediment in all very low; in fine, that they are all built of a porous stone, of a light or rather yellow gray, and in many places perforated and worn away" (Eustace, "Classical Tour").

Between the Temples of Ceres and Neptune remains of a Roman theatre and amphitheatre have been found, and other remains "lie round loose." The town walls of travertine were two miles round, and remains exist at various points. One gate still stands with dolphins and sirens on the key-stone.

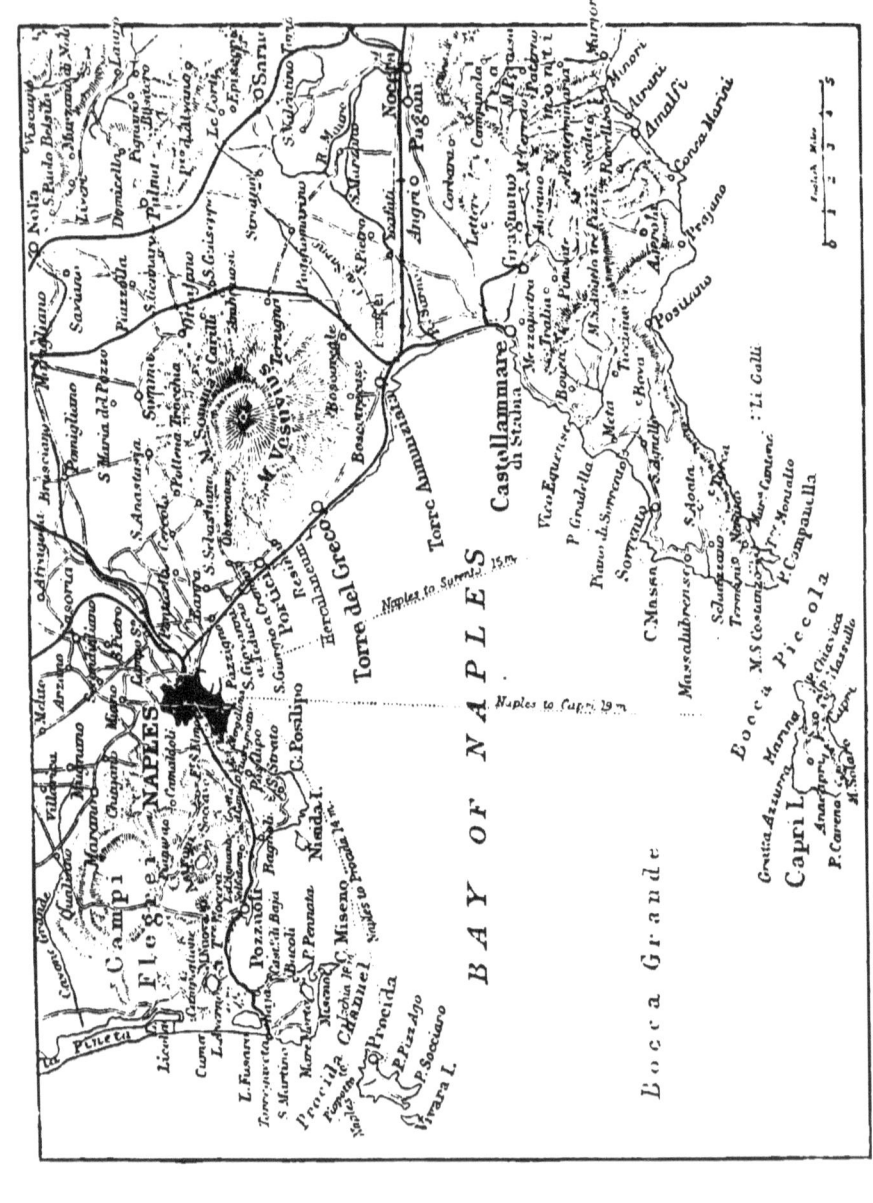

VISITOR'S NEAPOLITAN DIRECTORY.

ALPHABETICALLY ARRANGED.

ARTISTS.
NEAPOLITAN PAINTERS.

Cav. Sav. Altamura, 150 Rione Amedeo.
Consalvo Carelli, Palazzo Amodio, 4a Traversa Partenope.
Aslan d'Abro, Posilipo, Villa d'Abro.
Com. F. Maldarelli, Albergo dei Poveri.
Edoardo Dalbono, 70 Monteoliveto.
Cav. Mancini, 27 Strada Capodimonte.
Com. D. Morelli, Strada Pace, Palazzo Vonwiller.
Com. F. Palizzi, 1 Strada Ferrandina.
Cav. Netti, Arco Mirelli, Palazzo Capomazza.
Vincenzo Loria, 6 Via Vittoria.
Vincenco Caprile, 137 Corso Vittorio Emanuele.
Gustavo Mancinelli, 4a Traversa Partenope.
Vincenzo Volpe, 8 Vico S. Maria in Portico.

SOCIETÀ ARTISTICA NAPOLITANA,
190 Riviera di Chiaja, Palazzo Sirignano.
Permanent exhibition from 11 a.m. till 6 p.m. daily.

BATHS.

Bagni del Chiatamone, Strada Chiatamone. Warm baths (acqua dolce, di mare, ferruginosa), cold, shower, and swimming baths (even in winter) in a large basin with natural ferruginous water. of 12° to 15° Reaumur. Attached are Turkish and Pompeian Baths (Hammam).

Sea-Bathing in summer all along the bay, from establishments erected for the purpose. Those on Posilipo preferred, because the water is considerably cleaner.

BANKERS.

National Bank, Palazzo Maddaloni.
Bank of Naples, Palazzo S. Giacomo.
Holme & Co., 2 Via Flavio Gioja.
W. I. Turner & Co., 64 S. Lucia.
Meuricoffre & Co., 52 Piazza Municipio.
Thomas Cook & Sons, Piazza dei Martiri, Palazzo Partanna.

CARRIAGE FARES.

IN TOWN.	Daylight to Midnight.		Midnight to Daylight.	
	l.	c.	l.	c.
One-horse Cab (Carrozzelle).				
For the course..	0	70	1	10
For first hour...	1	50	2	10
For every extra hour.................................	1	10	1	50
Two-horse Carriage.				
For the course..	1	40	2	20
For first hour...	2	20	3	20
For every extra hour.................................	1	70	2	20

	One horse.		Two horses.	
OUT OF TOWN.	l.	c.	l.	c.
Posilipo	1	50	2	25
Fuorigrotta..	1	20	1	75
Bagnoli and Agnano................................	2	0	3	0
Vomero, Antignano, S. Martino.............	1	50	2	25
Capodimonte...	1	50	2	25
Miano and Marianella..............................	2	0	3	0
Piscinola...	2	50	3	75
Campo di Marte	1	50	2	25
Camposanto Nuovo..................................	1	50	2	25
Confalone...	1	10	1	65
Portici...	1	75	2	50
Resina...	2	0	3	0
Torre del Greco..	2	50	3	75
S. Giorgio a Cremano.............................	1	75	2	50
Barra...	1	75	2	20

N.B.—Always make a bargain when taking a carriage for any distance.

CHEMISTS.

THE INTERNATIONAL PHARMACY, via Calabritto, near Piazza dei Martiri.
DURST, Anglo-American Pharmacy, 31 Largo Garofalo a Chiaja.
D'EMILIO, 303 Via Roma.
KERNOT, 14 Strada S. Carlo.

CHURCHES (PROTESTANT).

Church of England (Christ Church), Strada S. Pasquale a Chiaja. Rev. HENRY T. BARFF, chaplain. Sundays, morning service, 11 A.M.; afternoon (from October to June), 3.45 P.M. Holy days, 11 A.M. Holy Communion, every Sunday (morning service).
French and German Evangelical Church, Strada Poerio a Chiaja già Vico Freddo, near Piazza dei Martiri.
Wesleyan Methodist Church and Schools, Vico S. Anna di Palazzo, Strada Chiaja. English service every Sunday morning at a quarter to eleven. Visitors are cordially invited, especially those English and Americans who are members of Methodist congregations.
Presbyterian Church, Strada Cappella Vecchia. Morning service, 11 A.M.; afternoon service (from October to June), 3.30 P.M. Prayer-meeting, Wednesday, 3 P.M. Communion on first Lord's day in January, March, May, July, September, November. Minister, Rev. THOS. JOHNSTONE IRVING, Free Church of Scotland.

CLUBS.

National Club, Largo Vittoria.
Casino dell' Unione, San Carlo Theatre.
Cerchio dell' Accademia, Piazza S. Ferdinando.

CONSULATES.

Austria-Hungary—Mr. RICCIARDI, 44 San' Anna dei Lombardi.
British Isles—Capt. HARTWELL, 4 Via Monte di Dio.
Belgium—4 Calata San Marco.
Denmark—Mr. CHRISTENSEN, 1 Vico Piliero.
France—Mr. POLLET, Via Vittoria, Palazzo Amodio.
Germany—V. REKOWSKI, 13 Via Pontano, Rione Amedeo.
Greece—Mr. GUDI, 255 Riviera di Chiaja.
Netherlands—Mr. MEURICOFFRE, 52 Via Municipio.
Portugal—41 Str. Egiziaca a Pizzofalcone.
Russia—30 Via Chiatamone.
Spain—32 Calata S. Bartolomeo.
Sweden and Norway—Mr. KLOUMANN, 15 Via Amedeo.

Switzerland—Mr. MEURICOFFRE, 52 Via Municipio.
Turkey—128 Rione Amedeo.
United States of America—Mr. TWELLS, 64 Santa Lucia.

DINING-ROOMS, RESTAURANTS.
(*Trattorie.*)
Birraria Gambrinus, corner of Chiaja and Piazza S. Ferdinando.
Restaurant Starace, Galleria Umberto I.
Birraria di Monaco, Piazza Municipio.
Al Vermouth di Torino, Via San Carlo, Galleria Umberto I.
Regina d'Italia, 319 Via Roma (1st floor).
Restaurant Continental, Strada Fontana Medina.
Giardini di Torino, 300 Via Roma (1st floor).
Santangelo, opposite the Museum, in Galleria Principe di Napoli.
Trattorie di Campagna, at Posilipo, on the Corso Vittorio Emanuele and on the Vomero. Fish dinners.

DOCTORS.
ENGLISH.
Dr. BARRINGER, 267 Riviera di Chiaja.
Dr. GAIRDNER, 128 Rione Amedeo.
Dr. JOHNSTON LAVIS, 7 Chiatamone.
Dr. MALBRANC, 145 Via Amedeo.
Dr. CHIARADIA (speaks English), 31 Via Bisignano.

ITALIAN.
Dr ARNALDO CANTANI, 23 Strada fuori Porta Medina.

DENTISTS.
Dr. ATKINSON (English), 228 Via Roma (Toledo).
Dr. KESSEL (Dane), 19 Via S. Caterina a Chiaja, near Piazza dei Martiri. Speaks English.

HOTELS.
Royal des Étrangers,
Victoria, Quay Partenope, } situated between Vittoria and S. Lucia, facing
Partenope-Métropole, } the sea, and offering good views of the bay and
Du Vésuve, } Vesuvius. Most convenient for sight-seeing.
De Russie,
Grande Bretagne, } opposite the Villa Nazionale.
De la Ville,
Grand Hotel Hauser, at the end of the Villa Gardens, near Torretta, facing the sea. Excellent.
West End Hotel, on the Rione Principe Amedeo.

West End (formerly Nobile), Rione Principe Amedeo.
Beaurivage,
Bristol,
Pension Britannique, on the Corso Vittorio Emanuele, in the upper part
Pension Belle Vue, of the town. Rather distant for sight-seers.
Tramontana-Parker,

LIBRARIES AND BOOKSELLERS.

Furchheim, 59 Piazza dei Martiri. Large stock of English, French, German, and Italian books, photographs, albums, and stationery. Author of the "Bibliografia di Pompei." Agent for Dr. Russell Forbes's publications. Information most willingly given to travellers.
Detken and Rocholl, Piazza Plebiscito.
Marghieri, Via Roma, Galleria Umberto I.
Pellerano, Via Gennaro Serra.
The University. Contains 25,000 volumes. Open from 9 to 3 P.M.
Biblioteca Nazionale. At the National Museum. Contains 200,000 volumes and 4,000 manuscripts.
Biblioteca Brancacciana. At S. Angelo a Nilo. It contains 70,000 volumes and 7,000 manuscripts.
Biblioteca S. Giacomo, Strada Concezione a Toledo.
Library of Gerolimini, opposite the Cathedral.
The Grandi Archivi, in the Convent of SS. Severino and Sossia, near the University.
Royal Academy of Archæology, Literature, and Fine Arts, at the University.
Accademia Pontaniana, Largo Donna Regina. Strada del Duomo.
Istituto d'Incoraggiamento of Technical Schools, Salita Tarsia.

MUSEUMS AND GALLERIES.

National Museum (*Museo Nazionale*). Open, May to October, from 9 till 3; November to April, from 10 till 4: charge, 1 lira; Sundays free.
Palazzo Fondi. Permission of the proprietors. (See p. 30.)
Filangieri (Industrial), Paggeria, behind Piazza Plebiscito.
Filangieri (Artistic and Antiquities), Strada del Duomo.

NAVIGATION.

Messageries Maritimes, 11-13 Strada Molo. Service from Marseilles to Turkey, Egypt, the Levant, India, China, and Japan.
Fraissinet, 3 Strada Piliero. Companies between Marseilles, Naples, and the Levant.
Peirano, 33 Strada Piliero.
Florio-Rubattino, 30 Via Piliero.
Anchor Line,
Cunard Line, } HOLME & Co., 2 Via Flavio Gioja.

Valery (French line), 1 Strada Piliero.
Capri and Ischia service, A. MANZI & Co., 34 Strado Molo Piccolo.

BOATS.

	l.	c.
Travellers coming from foreign places north of Italy or Sicily (with luggage or without)	1	0
From Salerno or Gaeta	0	40
From the islands of Capri, Ischia, Procida, or any place in the Bay of Naples	0	20

LUGGAGE.

	l.	c.
From the Molo to the carriage, one single trunk, not exceeding 100 kilos	0	40
Do., from 101 to 200 kilos	0	60
From the entrance, or station, and *vice versâ*, one single trunk of 100 kilos	0	20
Do., from 101 to 200 kilos	0	40
Small luggage (bags, hat-boxes, etc.)	0	20
One trunk from the post or station to the hotel, 100 kilos	1	0
Do., from 101 to 200 kilos	1	50

In case of any dispute with the boatman or coachman, it would be prudent to take the number and apply to the Questura, Piazza del Municipio, or to any of the municipal guards or police, whence one may obtain redress.

OMNIBUSES AND TRAMWAYS.

OMNIBUSES.

Piazza S. Ferdinando to—The Museum, Capodimonte, Post Office, Reclusorio, Vittoria, Mergellina, Funicolare del Vomero.

The different lines of omnibuses are easily distinguished by their colours, and names boldly painted on the sides.

The Piazza S. Ferdinando, on one side of the Royal Palace, may be taken as an omnibus and tramway centre.

TRAMWAYS.

(*Street Cars.*)

Post Office to Posilipo (by Piazza S. Ferdinando, S. Lucia, Vittoria, Riviera di Chiaja, and Mergellina).

Mergellina (Torretta) to Reclusorio (by Riviera di Chiaja, Vittoria, S. Lucia, Piazza S. Ferdinando, Strado Piliero, and Railway Station).

Piazza S. Ferdinando to Torre del Greco (by Portici and Resina).

Piazza S. Ferdinando to Porta Capuana and the Museum.

The Museum to Reclusorio and all the above points.

Fares:—First class, 15 to 50 centesimi; second class, 10 to 40 centesimi (according to distance).

STEAM TRAMS.

(*A Vapore.*)

Reclusorio to Caivano, Aversa.

Piazza S. Ferdinando to Pozzuoli, by way of Posilipo, by horse-cars, and thence through the new tunnel by steam.
Piedigrotta to the Museo (twenty-four trains daily), by Corso Vittorio Emanuele.

CABLE TRAMWAY.

(*Ferrovia Funicolare.*)

From Parco Margherita, on the Rione Amedeo, to Corso Vittorio Emanuele and Vomero. Also from Monte Santo, behind Piazza della Cartita, same direction.

ORDERS REQUIRED, AND WHERE OBTAINABLE.

Catacombs. Hospice of S. Gennaro.
Castle of S. Elmo. Commandant, Piazza del Plebiscito.
Palazzo Reale,
Capodimonte,
Caserta,
Favorita, of the Intendant, at the Royal Palace, Piazza del Plebiscito.
Quisisana,
Astroni,
Pompeii (for sketching). The Segreteria of the Museum at Naples.
Fondi Picture Gallery, Strada Medina.

Population—December 31st, 1891, 527,586; and 9,500 men garrison.
Post and Telegraph Offices—General Post Office, Monteoliveto, Palazzo Gravina. Letter-boxes cleared for France, England, Germany, Switzerland, Northern Italy, etc., at 9 and 11 A.M., at 12 noon, and at 1, 2, 3, 4, 5, and 8.30 P.M. *Branch Offices*—S. Lucia, Piazza S. Caterina a Chiaja, 147 Strada Foria, Railway station, Immacolatella (close to the port).
Telegrams—*Prices:* For the whole of Italy, 15 words, 1 lira ; for each extra word, 45 c. For foreign countries a word rate, after the initial payment of 1 lira. *Branch Offices*—Largo Garofalo a Chiaja, 42 Strada S. Giacomo, 108 Strada Foria.
Palace Cars, Pullman's—Agent : E. GRIMALDI, Strada Santa Brigida, Galleria Umberto I.
Police Office—Piazza Municipio, corner of Via Imbriani.
Shipping Agents—HOLME & Co., 2 Via Flavio Gioja ; ASELMEYER, PFISTER & Co., 34 Strada Piliero ; VICKERS & Co., 7 and 8 Via Vittoria.
Theatres—*S. Carlo*, near the Royal Palace. *Bellini*, Via Bellini. *Del Fondo*, Strada del Molo. *Fiorentini*, Strada Fiorentini. *Sannazaro*, Strada di Chiaja. *Nuovo*, Vico Lungo Teatro Nuovo. *Fenice*, Piazza del Municipio. *Rossini*, Salita Tarsia. *Politeama*, Strada Monte di Dio.
Water-Closets (*Latrine*)—Villa Nazionale, near the sea ; Strada Chiaja, in the staircase leading to Monte di Dio ; Piazza Plebiscito, on the western side of the colonnade ; Salita San Potito, near the Museum.

Index.

Agrippina's Tomb, 114.
Amalfi, 128.
Amphitheatres—
　Capua, 5.
　Cumæ, 108.
　Monte Cassino, 4.
　Pæstum, 134.
　Pompeii, 64.
　Puteoli, 107.
　Sorrento, 124.
Aquarium, 42.
Arch of Triumph, 33.
Arco Felice, 107.
Artists, 135.

Bacoli, 114.
Bagnoli, 101.
Baiæ, 111.
Bankers, 136.
Basilica Augustalis, 36.
Baths, Ancient, 37.
Baths, Modern, 135.
Baths of Nero, 111.
Baths of Tiberius, 120.
Bay of Naples, 118.
Boats, 140.
Booksellers, 139.
Bridge of Caligula, 103.

Camaldoli, 87.
Capodimonte, 7, 28.
Capri, 118.
Carriage fares, 136.
Castel del Carmine, 34
Castellamare, 126.
Castello dell' Ovo, 8.
Castel Nuovo, 33.
Castel S. Elmo, 7, 38.
Catacombs, 28.
Cento Camerelle, 114.

Chemists, 137.
Churches—
　Domenico Maggiore, 29.
　Gesù Nuovo, 28.
　L'Incoronata, 30.
　Protestant, 137.
　S. Anna de' Lombardi, 30.
　SS. Apostoli, 34.
　S. Barbara, 34.
　S. Chiara, 29.
　S. Francesco di Paola, 8.
　S. Gennaro, 28.
　S. Giacomo degli Spagnuoli, 33.
　S. Januarius, 36.
　S. Lorenzo Maggiore, 36.
　S. Maria del Carmine, 34
　S. Martino, 37.
　S. Paolo Maggiore, 35.
　S. Restituta, 37.
　S. Severo, 29.
City of the dead: Impressions, 83.
Clubs, 137.
Consulates, 137.
Corso Vittorio Emanuele, 38.
Cumæ, 108.

Dentists, 138.
Destruction of Pompeii, 46.
Dining-Rooms, 138.
Directory, 135.
Doctors, 138.

Elysian Fields, 87, 115.
Environs, 43; Map of, 134-5.

Fountains--
　Charles III., 30.

Fountains—
　Medina, 33.
　S. Lucia, 8.

Galleria Principe di Napoli, 9.
Galleria Umberto, 33.
Galleries, Picture, 139.
Grottoes—
　Blue, 120.
　D'Averno, 110.
　Della Pace, 109.
　Di Cane, 100.
　Posilipo, 98.
　Sejanus, 110.
　Sibyl, 108, 110.

Hadrian to his soul, 106.
Herculaneum, 94.
Historical notices—
　Capri, 122.
　Herculaneum, 95.
　Pompeii, 46.
　Vesuvius, 89.
Hotels, 138.
How to see Naples, xi.

International Hospital, 38.

Lakes—
　Agnano, 100.
　Avernus, 109.
　Fusaro, 114.
　Lucrinus, 109.
Libraries, 139.
Luggage, 140.

Map to Naples, 6, 7.
Misenum, 115.
Monte Nuovo, 107.

INDEX.

Monte Solaro, 120.
Museum, National, 10.
Museum, S. Martino, 37.
Museums, 139.

Naples, 7.
Naples: How to see it, xi.
Naples a Roman colony, 31.
Navigation, 139.
Neapolitan Life, 30.
Nisida, 115.

Omnibuses, 140.
Orders required, 141.

Pæstum, 87, 130.
Palaces—
  Astroni, 100.
  Capodimonte, 28.
  Fondi, 30.
  La Favorita, 97.
  Royal, 9.
Palæopolis, 7.
Parthenope, 7.
Paul's landing-place, 103.
Phlegræan Fields, 87, 115.
Piazzas—
  Dante, 9.
  Dei Martiri, 32.
  Del Municipio, 33.
  Del Plebiscito, 8.
  Ferdinando, 9.
Piscina Mirabilis, 115.
Pizzofalcone, 8.
Police office, 141.
Pompeii, 43.
Population, 141.
Porta Alba, 9.
Porta Capuana, 34.

Portici, 88.
Posilipo, 98.
Postal notices, 141.
Puteoli, 102.
Puzzuoli, 102.

Railways, 6, 101.
Rambles in Naples, ix.
Ramble through the city of the dead, 52, 83.
Resina, 88.
Restaurants, 138.
Riviera di Chiaja, 42.
Route—Rome to Naples, 1.

Salerno, 128.
School of Virgil, 117.
Serapeum, 104.
Shipping agents, 141.
S. Lucia, 8.
Solfatara, 100.
Sorrento, 124.
Stufe di Nerone, 111.
Stufe di San Germano, 100.

Telegrams, 141.
Temples—
  Apollo, 109.
  Augustus, 102.
  Castor and Pollux, 35, 133.
  Ceres, 132.
  Diana, 102, 113.
  Giants, 108.
  Mercury, 34, 113.
  Mithras, 120.
  Neptune, 104, 133.
  Nymphs, 104.
  Serapis, 104.
  Venus, 112.

Theatres—
  Ancient Herculaneum, 96.
  Ancient Pæstum, 134.
  Ancient Pompeii, 63.
  Ancient Puteoli, 106.
  Ancient Roman, 35.
  Modern, 141.
  S. Carlo, 32.
Tomb of Agrippina, 114.
Tomb of Virgil, 40.
Torre del Greco, 43.
Torre dell' Annunziata, 43.
Tramways, 140.
Triumphal Arch, 33.

Useful hints, xii.
Useful information, 135.

Vesuvius, 88.
Via Herculea, 110.
Via Roma, 9.
Villas—
  Cæsar, 114.
  Cicero's Pompeian, 81.
  Cicero's Puteolaneum, 104.
  Donn' Anna, 117.
  La Favorita, 97.
  Lucullus, 116.
  Nazionale, 42.
  Pollius Felix, 124.
  Quisisana, 126.
  Sans Souci, 117.
  Servilius Vatia, 102, 114.
  Tiberius, 120.
  Vedius Pollio, 116.
  Virgil, 117.
Virgil's Tomb, 40.

Water Supply, xii.

Index to Pompeii.

Amphitheatre, 64.
Arch of Nero, 70.

Basilica, 56.
Baths, Public, 70.
Baths, Stabian, 66.
Bibliografia, 44.

Chalcidicum, 60.
Curia Isiaca, 63.

Destruction of Pompeii, 46.

Forum, Great, 58.
Forum, Triangular, 62.

Gate, Herculaneum, 79.
Gate, Sea, 53.
Gladiators' barracks, 63.
Guild hall of fullers, 60.

Hall of town council, 60.
Historical notices, 46.
Houses—
  Abbondanza, 68.
  Arbaces, 70.
  Bear, 67.
  Centenario, 67.
  Cornelius Rufus, 64.
  Epidius Rufus, 66.

INDEX.

Houses—
  Faun, 70.
  Fontana in Musaico, 68.
  Gladiators, 62.
  Glaucus, 74
  Holconius, 62.
  Ione, 70.
  Large Mosaic Fountain, 74.
  Lucius Cæcilius Jucundus, 69.
  Marcus Lucretius, 67.
  Orpheus, 69.
  Pansa, 74.
  Poets, 69.
  Sallust, 79.
  Small Mosaic Fountain, 74.
  Specchio, 68.
  Tragic Poet, 74.
  Vestals, 79.

Impressions, 83.

Latest Excavations, 62, 69.
Law Courts, 62.

Map, Large, 53, 54.
Map, Sketch, 45.
Masonic Lodge, 64.
Museum, 53.

Pantheon, 60.
Pliny's letters to Tacitus, 46.
Pompeii: how to get there, etc., 43.
Porta Marina, 53.
Porta Stabiana, 63.

Ramble through the City of the Dead, 52, 83.
Recent Excavations, 67, 69.

Regioni, 53.

Street of Abundance, 62.
Street of the Balcony, 85.
Street of Sallust, 77.
Street of Tombs, 79.

Temples—
  Benign Jupiter, 64.
  Fortune, 70.
  Hercules, 62.
  Isis, 62.
  Jupiter, 58.
  Mercury, 60.
  Venus, 58.
Theatre, Comic, 63.
Theatre, Tragic, 63.
Tombs, 79.

Villa of Cicero, 81.
Villa of Diomedes, 81.

www.ingramcontent.com/pod-product-compliance
Lightning Source LLC
Chambersburg PA
CBHW030246170426
43202CB00009B/643